RISK
AND
CULTURE

RISK
AND
CULTURE

An Essay on the Selection

of Technical and Environmental Dangers

———

MARY DOUGLAS

and

AARON WILDAVSKY

UNIVERSITY OF CALIFORNIA PRESS

BERKELEY   LOS ANGELES   LONDON

University of California Press
Berkeley and Los Angeles, California

University of California Press, Ltd.
London, England

First Paperback Printing 1983
ISBN 0-520-05063-0

Library of Congress Cataloging in Publication Data

Douglas, Mary.
    Risk and culture.

    Includes index.
    1. Risk.   I. Wildavsky, Aaron B.   II. Title.
H91.D68   304   81-16318
                                   AACR2

Printed in the United States of America

1 2 3 4 5 6 7 8 9

For Dean Neubauer
who brought us together

Contents

Acknowledgments		ix
Introduction:	Can We Know the Risks We Face?	1
I	Risks are Hidden	16
II	Risks are Selected	29
III	Scientists Disagree	49
IV	Assessment is Biased	67
V	The Center is Complacent	83
VI	The Border is Alarmed	102
VII	The Border Fears for Nature	126
VIII	America is a Border Country	152
IX	The Dialogue is Political	174
Conclusion:	Risk is a Collective Construct	186
Notes		199
Index		215

Acknowledgments

This book is based upon research supported by the National Science Foundation under Grant No. ERS77-15503 and by the Russell Sage Foundation. Any opinions, findings, and conclusions or recommendations expressed in this publication are those of the authors and do not necessarily reflect the views of the National Science Foundation or the Russell Sage Foundation. Our appreciation goes to the two foundations for their financial support. Andrée Breaux, Steve Rayner, and Katherine Riggs provided outstanding research assistance on environmental groups; their contributions are noted in the relevant chapters. The word "indispensable" would apply only to our secretaries, Doris Patton in Berkeley and Madge Spitaleri in New York.

We have been fortunate in our readers; valuable advice has been offered us even if we did not always accept it or if the commentator did not agree with our approach. Our thanks go to Peter D'Eustachio, Yaron Ezrahi, Ernst Haas, William Havender, C. S. Holling, Howard Kunreuther, William Lowrance, Giandomenico Majone, Ted Marmor, Joshua Menkes, John Miles, Robert Mitchell, Dorothy Nelkin, Julian Simon, Arthur Stinchcombe, Michael Thompson, and Carol Weisbrod.

To each other we give the two essential acknowledgments of collaboration: we believe this book is better than either of us could have done alone; indeed, unless we had done it together, we could not have done it at all.

But wretched Man is still in arms for Fear.

From fear to fear, successively betrayed—
By making risks to give a cause for fear
(Feeling safe with causes, and from birth afraid)

—William Empson, *Reflection from Rochester*

Introduction:

Can We Know The Risks
We Face?

Can we know the risks we face, now or in the future? No, we cannot; but yes, we must act as if we do. Some dangers are unknown; others are known, but not by us because no one person can know everything. Most people cannot be aware of most dangers at most times. Hence, no one can calculate precisely the total risk to be faced. How, then, do people decide which risks to take and which to ignore? On what basis are certain dangers guarded against and others relegated to secondary status?

The current consideration of risk has three peculiarities. The first is that disagreement about the problem is deep and widespread in the Western world. The second is that different people worry about different risks—war, pollution, employment, inflation. The third is that knowledge and action are out of sync: whatever programs are enacted to reduce risks, they conspicuously fail to follow the principle of doing the most to prevent the worst damage.[1] In sum, substantial disagreement remains over what is risky, how risky it is, and what to do about it.

Are dangers really increasing or are we more afraid? Undoubtedly people and the environment face risks from technology. The perils of nuclear wastes and carcinogenic chemicals are not figments of the imagination. Undoubtedly, also, we benefit from technology. Life expectancy continues to increase; accident rates and infant mortality are way down. Are the dangers worth the advances? Do we make too much or too little of such risks and benefits? Different groups give exposure to toxic chemicals vastly different significance. Fear of risk, coupled with the confidence to face it, has something to do with knowledge and something to do with the kind of people we are.

At the level of public policy the main dangers can be grouped into four kinds:

1. foreign affairs: the risk of foreign attack or encroachment; war; loss of influence, prestige, and power;
2. crime: internal collapse; failure of law and order; violence versus white collar crime;
3. pollution: abuse of technology; fears for the environment; and
4. economic failure: loss of prosperity.

Do those people who worry about the future worry equally about all four kinds of risk? A Harris survey on attitudes about risk — among the general public, corporate executives, and federal regulators — demonstrates the diversity of perspectives. The Harris findings show that twice as many people in the general public (as compared to executives) think that there is more risk in society today than 20 years ago. As for domestic political instability, 61 percent of both the public and executives feel there is more risk; but only 34 percent of the regulators agree with this. In regard to danger from the chemicals in use, however, almost 3 times as many executives (38 percent) as the general public and the regulators (13 percent each) think there is *less* risk today than 20 years before. Comparing regulators to executives, 41 percent of the latter felt the greatest risks facing the country (in March 1980) were the economy and energy; only 10 percent of federal regulators gave the same response.[2]

At the elite level of public debate, the actors — political parties, interest groups, government officials — do not uniformly attach the same dangers to different objects. People who are most concerned about attack from abroad, for instance, tend to be less worried about pollution at home. Those who would take strong steps to counter violent crime in the streets are not as passionate about the effects of inequality of income. Why not? The two trends may well be connected.

The mark of an intelligent man, it is said, is that the more he learns, the more he becomes aware of how much more there is to know. The advance of science increases human understanding of the natural world. By opening up new realms of knowledge, however, science simultaneously can increase the gap between what is known and what it is desirable to know.

What would be needed to make us able to understand the risks that face us? — Nothing short of total knowledge (a mad answer to an impossible question). The hundreds of thousands of chemicals about whose dangers so much is said are matched easily by the diversity of the causes of war or the afflictions of poverty or the horrors of religious and racial strife. Just trying to think of what categories of objects a person might be concerned about is alarming. Indeed, it might be better for mental health to limit rather than expand sources of concern. Since no one can attend to everything, some sort of priority must be established among dangers; otherwise, merely counting risky objects would leave us defenseless.

Ranking dangers (which is what risk assessment requires) so as to know which ones to address and in what order, demands prior agreement on criteria. There is no mechanical way to produce a ranking. As Jerome R. Ravetz, a philosopher of science, puts it:

The hope that one can produce a taxonomy, evaluation, and finally a technical fix to the problems of risks is in substance as ambitious as the program of putting all of human experience and value onto a scale of measurement for mathematical or political manipulation.[3]

Because no one knows it all, there can be no guarantee that the very dangers people seek to avoid are those that actually will harm them most. Moreover, successful surmounting of one danger is not always a good omen. Success may lead people to relax their guard in overcoming adversity. Then, the next unexpected danger may do them in. As Ravetz reminds us,

risks are conceptually uncontrollable; one can never know whether one is doing *enough* to prevent a hazard from occurring. Even after a hazard has occurred, one is still left with the question of how much more action would have been necessary to have prevented it, and whether such action would have been within the bounds of "reasonable" behavior.[4]

Even in the distant future, when the record of these times is more complete, historians undoubtedly will differ about whether our generation might have taken different, safer paths. Yet, act we must, not knowing what will happen to us along the path we choose to take.

When one enlarges the question to ask about which kinds of risks are acceptable to what sorts of people—the prime political question—the uncertainties surrounding current knowledge are multiplied. A comprehensive study of acceptable risk by Baruch Fischhoff, Sarah Lichtenstein, and Paul Slovic concludes that acceptability is always a political issue:

That choice depends upon the alternatives, values, and beliefs that are considered. As a result, there is no single all-purpose number that expresses "acceptable risk" for a society.

Values and uncertainties are an integral part of every acceptable-risk problem. As a result, there are no value-free processes for choosing between risky alternatives. The search for an "objective method" is doomed to failure and may blind the searchers to the value-laden assumptions they are making. . . .

Not only does each approach fail to give a definitive answer, but it is predisposed to representing particular interests and recommending particular solutions. Hence, choice of a method is a political decision with a distinct message about who should rule and what should matter.[5]

Since there is no single correct conception of risk, there is no way to get everyone else to accept "it."

No person can know more than a fraction of the dangers that abound. To believe otherwise is to believe that we know (or can know) everything. Yet even if we did, it would still be necessary for us to agree on a ranking of risks. In the absence of complete knowledge, and in the presence of disagreement between scientists and laymen alike, how can anyone choose to zero in on any particular set of dangers? How, faced with endless possibilities, can anyone calculate the probabilities of harm (the risks)?

Risk should be seen as a joint product of *knowledge* about the future and *consent* about the most desired prospects. This enables us to put the problems into perspective.

CHART A

Four Problems of Risk

Knowledge

		Certain	Uncertain
Consent	Complete	Problem: *Technical* Solution: *Calculation*	Problem: *Information* Solution: *Research*
	Contested	Problem: (*dis*)*Agreement* Solution: *Coercion* or *Discussion*	Problem: *Knowledge* and *Consent* Solution: ?

When knowledge is certain and consent complete, when objectives are agreed and all alternatives (together with the probability of occurrence) are known, a program can be written to produce the best solution. The problem is technical and the solution is one of calculation. In the next instance — knowledge certain, but consent contested — the problem is one of disagreement about how to value consequences; here the solution is either more coercion or more discussion. In the third case, complete consent hampered by uncertain knowledge leads to the problem of risk being defined as insufficient information; hence the solution is seen as research. Looking at the way governments handle controversies over risk in Europe and America, Nelkin and Pollak observe:

> If lack of confidence is thought to be a problem arising from insufficient technical evidence, then the goal is to ascertain "scientific truth." This leads to a structure based on scientific advice to public representatives. If the controversy is defined in terms of alienation, a more participatory or consultative system is developed. And if the problem of public consensus is defined in terms of inadequate information, it is assumed that people oppose technologies because they are poorly informed. The task then becomes one of "education."[6]

The last situation, in which knowledge is uncertain and consent is contested, is precisely how any informed person would characterize the contemporary dilemma of risk assessment.

What can reduce the need for new knowledge and at the same time focus attention on a few critical subjects? Only social consent keeps an issue out of contention. The perception of risk is a social process. All society depends on combinations of confidence and fear. Learning about fear ought to afford a backdoor route for understanding confidence. Some fears are physical, some are social. Perhaps physical fears would not threaten to overwhelm citizens who felt confident of justice and social support. Perhaps people are not so much afraid of dying as afraid of death without honor. In addressing questions of acceptable risk without considering their social aspects, we could be speaking to the wrong problems.

The different social principles that guide behavior affect the judgment of what dangers should be most feared, what risks are worth taking, and who should be allowed to take them. In Zaire the Lele people suffered all the usual devastating tropical ills — fever, gastroenteritis, tuberculosis, leprosy, ulcers, barrenness, and pneumonia. In this world of disease, they focused mainly on being struck by lightning, the affliction of barrenness, and one disease, bronchitis; they mainly attributed these troubles to specific types of immorality in which the victim would generally be seen as innocent and some powerful leader or village elder would be blamed. In other countries the prevailing culture promotes a different selection from a similar range of hazards. Sometimes, instead of pinning the blame on the village elders, it rather enhances self-blame: in those cases a disaster is the victim's own fault. Whether blaming the elders or blaming the victim, the type of society generates the type of accountability and focuses concern on particular dangers. Much as in biology, the cultural theory of risk perception which will be developed in these pages sees the social environment, the selection principles, and the perceiving subject as all one system. It does not ignore the reality of the dangers around. Plenty of real dangers are always present. No doubt the water in fourteenth century Europe was a persistent health hazard, but a cultural theory of perception would point out that it became a public preoccupation only when it seemed plausible to accuse Jews of poisoning the wells.

A cultural approach can make us see how community consensus relates some natural dangers to moral defects. According to this argument, dangers are selected for public concern according to the strength and direction of social criticism. Death and disease statistics are mobilized for justifying the criticism. Why is asbestos poisoning seen to be more fearsome than fire? Asbestos was developed to save people from burning; asbestos poisoning is a form of industrial pollution whose toll of deaths by cancer justifies a particular anti-industrial criticism more strongly than does loss of life by fire. Similarly, there is no obvious way in which the incidence of skin cancer caused by leisure-time sunburn can be mobilized for criticism of industry, and so we hear less of it. We shall show that this connection between perceived risk and moral blame does not reduce the selection of dangers to political analysis. At the same time politics must not be avoided. A cultural theory of risk perception would be trivial if it shirked considering the distribution of power in relation to the pattern of risks incurred by Americans. Our guiding assumptions are that any form of society produces its own selected view of the natural environment, a view which influences its choice of dangers worth attention. Attribution of responsibility for natural disasters is a normal strategy for protecting a particular set of values belonging to a particular way of life. Consequently, research into risk perception based on a cultural model would try to discover what different characteristics of social life elicit different responses to danger.

This book is about how particular kinds of danger come to be selected for attention. We could have chosen to discuss perception of the risks of poverty or of war, but it is not an encyclopedia. Our book is about why, at this time, pollution has been singled out for special concern. Our answer will be that the choice of risks to worry about depends on the social forms selected. The choice of risks and the choice of how to live are taken together. Each form of social life has its own typical risk portfolio. Common values lead to common fears (and, by implication, to a common agreement not to fear other things). There is no gap between perception and reality and no correct description of the right behavior, at least not in advance. The real dangers are not known until afterward (there always being alternative hypotheses). In the meantime, acting in the present to ward off future dangers, each social arrangement elevates some risks to a high peak and depresses others below sight. This cultural bias[7] is integral to social organization. Risk taking and risk aversion, shared confidence and shared fears, are part of the dialogue on how best to organize social relations. For to organize means to organize some things *in* and other things *out*. When we say, therefore, that a certain kind of society is biased toward stressing the risk of pollution, we are not saying that other kinds of social organization are objective and unbiased but rather that they are biased toward finding different kinds of dangers.

How do we choose which risks to face? We choose the risks in the same package as we choose our social institutions. Since an individual cannot look in all directions at once, social life demands organization of bias. People order their universe through social bias. By bringing these biases out into the open, we will understand better which policy differences can be reconciled and which cannot.

Each side in the current risk debate is thought by the other to be serving interests of preferred social institutions. Whether the reference is to the industrial establishment or the "danger establishment" that lobbies against it, each takes the arguments of the other to be self-serving and therefore false. Cultural bias is much more complicated. What to do about it depends, first and foremost, on learning to recognize it.

To ask which is the correct description of rational behavior (that is, to ask what the real risks are) leads to an answer which finds irrational bias and misperceptions of real interest in the viewpoint of anyone who disagrees. Instead, cultural analysis shows how a given cluster of values and beliefs makes sense out of the various positions people take and the practices they employ. To what beliefs and values would members of society most readily refer in order for that kind of society to have credible, coherent institutions?

Once the idea is accepted that people select their awareness of certain dangers to conform with a specific way of life, it follows that people who adhere to different forms of social organization are disposed to take (and avoid) different kinds of risk. To alter risk selection and risk perception, then, would depend on changing the social organization.

Questions about acceptable levels of risk can never be answered just by explaining how nature and technology interact. What needs to be explained is how people agree to ignore most of the potential dangers that surround them and interact so as to concentrate only on selected aspects.

Let us try it another way: the key terms in the debate over technology are risk and acceptability. In calculating the probability of danger from technology, one concentrates on the risk that is physically "out there," in man's intervention in the natural world. In determining what is acceptable, one concentrates on the uncertainty that is "in here," within a person's mind. Going from "out there" to "in here" requires a connection between the dangers of technology and people's perception of those risks. Neither the one approach (that the perils of technology are objectively self-evident) nor the other (that all perceptions are subjective) can connect the two. Only a cultural approach can integrate moral judgments about how to live with empirical judgments about what the world is like.

To develop the argument, we turn to a cultural change that has taken place in our own generation. We begin with a sense of wonder. Try to read a newspaper or news magazine, listen to radio, or watch television; on any day some alarm bells will be ringing. What are Americans afraid of? Nothing much, really, except the food they eat, the water they drink, the air they breathe, the land they live on, and the energy they use. In the amazingly short space of fifteen to twenty years, confidence about the physical world has turned into doubt. Once the source of safety, science and technology have become the source of risk. What could have happened in so short a time to bring forth so severe a reaction? How can we explain the sudden, widespread, across-the-board concern about environmental pollution and personal contamination that has arisen in the Western world in general and with particular force in the United States?

Our argument is that a complex historical pattern of social changes has led to values that we identify as sectarian being more widely espoused. The sectarian outlook has three positive commitments: to human goodness, to equality, to purity of heart and mind. The dangers to the sectarian ideal are worldliness and conspiracy. Put into secular terms, worldliness appears in big organization, big money, and market values— all deny equality and attack goodness and purity; conspiracy includes factions plotting secret attack, transporting evil into an essentially good world. Infiltration from the evil world appears as Satanism, witchcraft, or their modern equivalent—

hidden technological contamination that invades the body of nature and of man. We shall argue that these ideals and these dangers respond to the problems of voluntary organization: they are the daily coinage of debate in groups that are trying to hold their members together without coercion or overt leadership. The remedies most easily proposed in such organizations are to refuse to compromise with evil and to root it out, accompanied by a tendency toward intolerance and drastic solutions. These organizations depending on the voluntary principle also tend to reject wealth. Nature in the wild, uncorrupted by social artifice, equivalent to a society without social distinction, is their preferred emblem of godliness and symbol of unworldliness. Before developing this cultural explanation of the current directions of risk aversion, we should consider some rival theories.

A favorite explanation for the intense new interest in risk is that the United States is richer and Americans can now afford to be more cautious. Lester Lave writes:

Although no evidence exists that Americans have become sated with the products of the U.S. industrial economy, it is natural that they should want a more pleasant environment, lower risks associated with their products and work places, and general health improvements to accompany their increases in real income. What appears to be a paradox ["that Americans are safer now than ever before, but at the same time they are more concerned about health and safety than ever before"] is resolved by recognizing the rapidly increasing desire for lower risk.[8]

After all, this argument runs, the more people have, the more they can lose. Once people have satisfied their main material wants, from cars to television, they can concern themselves with safety. So far as it goes, this explanation is plausible. We do more for self-protection because we are able to do it. Safety is presented as another consumer good, part of general material advance. But is it true that richer people are more averse to risk? If that is so, why are they not risk averse to economic disaster, crime, and war? Why do they select technological rather than other kinds of risks? Even more fundamentally, why should the success of a way of life generate self-doubt among its adherents? Success could more likely be expected to generate confidence in more of the same. The problem is not merely a rise in the value of safety. There is the proposition that affluence has bred distrust of the culture that created it. Where does this idea come from?

The proliferation of research on risk has called forth various sociological theories about the sources of public concern. Divisions among the general public are scanned to see whether changes in income, education, or rural and urban dwelling patterns can account for changing public judgments. It is reported that public-interest groups tend to be run by individuals in the professional and managerial occupations with higher-than-average income and education. More to the point — this is true of leaders everywhere — their rank and file are more educated than is the general public.[9] Such observations lead to a variant of this explanation: education itself has bred a social conscience.

It is plausible that the most alert watchdogs on behalf of society should come from the most educated classes. But this in itself does not explain why the last twenty years should have seen the change and why concern should take this particular direction. For education to explain the new attitudes toward risk, one would need to indicate some threshold at which the educated elite tips over from unconcern to concern. This is provided by Maslow's theory of stages of wants.[10] When struggling for bare survival, according to Maslow, the individual has a narrow perspective; his political demands are material, for food and shelter. With industrial wealth guaranteeing economic well-being, the individual looks around for forms of personal expression and personal freedom. At a more developed stage of the economy, the individual can afford the luxury of a social conscience; at this point altruistic concerns come to the surface. Hence the growth of public interest lobbies, and so on. Still this does not explain the selection of risks. Why is social conscience concerned with environment and not with the education of the poor or relief of the indigent?

Since they no longer need to worry about the safety or sustenance of their bodies, the educated public can presumably satisfy what Ronald Inglehart calls nonmaterial needs for group identification and for self-realization.[11] Their aims are not for more income, but for a high quality of life, including democratization of work. At this stage what people most want is a sense of individual control over social forces. This want is so imperious that their demands tend to be "non-negotiable."[12] Thus Inglehart uses Maslow's stages to explain a new era of public sensitivity to oppression and of concern for fellow men on an international scale of comparison. The idea is pleasing. It supposes that the social classes least motivated by concern for public welfare are only those less prosperous. All people would be speaking for the public interest if they were fortunate enough to have solved their material and money needs. One might naturally expect public-interest groups to concentrate on spreading prosperity. Psychology, however, seems to be against the theory; so does history. It is easy to think of extravagantly affluent civilizations where the elites were not at all public-spirited.

Maslow's argument supposes that a mood of public altruism is generated by the sheer material successes of industrial development. The empirical difficulty is that altruism is not a post-industrial monopoly. Most nonindustrialized cultures have their equivalent of public-interest watchdogs, however low their level of poverty. It is hard to name a time in the last 100 years, moreover, when Western industrialized society was not rich enough to qualify for the last altruistic phase, whose predominance among us now needs to be explained. What is it about affluence now and security now that is different? According to our argument, advanced technology is not the explanation. There is no unequivocal body of evidence that life is (or is becoming) less safe; on the contrary, such tentative evidence as there is leads in the opposite direction—life is growing longer not shorter; health is better not worse. We get more insight from asking why certain risks get selected from the range of dangers that always threaten. This question points to the growth of sectarianism as a more convincing answer.

The organization of this book reflects the kind of question we ask: What sort of people would use risks to nature to get other people to change their ways? If we asked, "What has modern technology done to nature to cause so much concern?", we would concentrate on evaluating the scientific evidence about environmental damage. Instead we begin by analyzing the arguments connecting technology to environmental decline — risks are hidden, involuntary, and irreversible — in order to show that the judgments are essentially social rather than scientific. One response to this thesis is that we modern people see things differently precisely because we share an empirical, evidential, scientific ethos. In order to show that risks are socially selected, in our second chapter we compare "advanced" views with those of "primitive" peoples. Readers are welcome to see if they can discern differences between "us" and "them" in the way that dangers are selected for public concern. Even if we were all scientists, the third chapter shows, we would be no nearer agreement because scientists themselves are as divided on risk as are the rest of us. Nor will the procedures of risk assessment help in this regard, the fourth chapter asserts, because all modes of assessment are biased by the social assumptions they make. Having done our best to dispose of the contention that selection of dangers could be determined by direct assessment of the physical evidence, we begin to develop the case for social selection of risk. Chapters five through seven argue that each culture, each set of shared values and supporting social institutions, is biased toward highlighting certain risks and downplaying others. Along the way, we mix examples of risk selection among people like ourselves and people such as the Amish and the Hutterites, contemporaries who have a strange appearance to the modern eye. One reason for doing this is that these peoples and their cultures have a pronounced identity, so they can be readily described. A more important reason lies at the heart of our position: If risk and culture are related in the ways we claim, then these relationships should stand out among the most diverse people way back when and not only among us moderns here and now. Since this is a book that explicitly aims to explain us to ourselves by making explicable heretofore puzzling phenomena—the rise of alarm over risk to life at the same time as health is better than ever before —we go on to apply our cultural theory to American conditions. We end by considering the policy implications of the cultural selection of dangers, denying that it forces us to adopt an unscientific posture and affirming our capacity to cope resiliently with risk.

I

Risks are Hidden

If we ask why in the United States today there is an urgent, massive, collective concern to ward off risk, we receive seemingly straightforward answers. The human race and its physical environment is threatened with degradation or even extinction. What is more, the risks are so great that no knowledgeable individual would accept them. What is worse, the risks are the more insidious for being kept secret. Decomposing this impending catastrophe into its essential elements, we are being told that the dangers are involuntary (we would not willingly accept them), irreversible (there is no turning back), and hidden (we shall not know we are encountering them). The fear is that the effects of technology may prove disastrous.

INVOLUNTARY RISKS

There is a prima facie plausibility in assuming that individuals make a strong distinction between risks that they undertake knowingly and risks that are imposed on them. In other words, they are philosophical about damage they incur through their own fault or through choice of dangerous sports, drinks, foods. They know that at the age of fifty, if they want longevity, they should not overeat or drink too much liquor, but that is their affair. What makes them understandably angry is damage that they feel they should have been warned against, that they might have avoided had they known, damage caused by other people, particularly people profiting from their innocence. The attitude corresponds closely to legal conceptions of employers' liability and the responsibility of producers to sell safe goods. The force of the distinction for public policy is that the rights of free individuals are not to be restricted but neither is their environment to be laden with risks unbeknown to them. The general argument also provides a plausible explanation of the shift in public attitudes toward danger. If people are being increasingly deprived of control over their own lives, if the march of big bureaucracy incorporates yearly larger proportions of the population in its ranks, if people feel helpless— then their sense of outrage at involuntary risks will naturally grow more intense. The argument also suggests a solution. Its main protagonist, Chauncey Starr, by developing a form of risk-benefit analysis, claims to provide an objective tool for measuring the expected dangers against the expected benefits of new technology, thus enabling cool, politically neutral decisions to be made and, better still, to be justified before the legislature. But unfortunately, the distinction between the voluntary and involuntary incurring of danger is not objectively identifiable.

If you and I want to go rock climbing, thus voluntarily exposing ourselves to risks, presumably that is our own business and that would be all right. But if the air contains coal dust or food contains carcinogens, that would be all wrong because the risk to us is involuntary. At first blush, the distinction appears eminently reasonable; there are indeed risks additional to the standardized risk of daily living that individuals are allowed to assume voluntarily (though there are always some others, such as climbing the outside of skyscrapers, that are prohibited). There are also risks that are unknown. It is obvious that people may and do endanger themselves (and, possibly, others around them) without realizing that what they are doing or what is being done near them is dangerous. The remedy, equally obvious, is better information. People will either refuse a known risk or seek additional compensation for assuming it. Thus an involuntary risk due to ignorance is by knowledge converted into one that is averted or into a voluntary risk.

No doubt there are risks that we would rather not run but that we undertake in order to gain other benefits. People do live in Los Angeles, for example, not for the privilege of breathing in smog but in order to take advantage of its natural beauty, warm climate, job opportunities, and so on. Life's choices, after all, often come in bundles of goods and bads, which have to be taken whole. There is no sense in acting as if one can pick the eyes out of the potato of life, making entirely discrete choices, when it comes all tied up, the bad with the good inextricably mixed.

Unwanted it may be. In all frankness, the risk that comes with the reward can hardly be called involuntary. The term would be appropriate only when there is some compulsion. Yet there is a limit to which the term compulsion can be stretched without changing the argument.

The distribution of life chances through any society are hardly equal. Some classes of people face greater risks than others. Poorer people, on the average, are sicker than rich, die earlier, have more accidents. We cannot say that all classes of people who incur greater risk in the course of their lives incur it voluntarily. A person might prefer to risk an industrial accident, or accept a certain degree of pollution, to being unemployed; the risk incurred is involuntary in the special sense that people would rather things were otherwise. The risks they face may be unwelcome and against their will; they would not accept them if they were rich or beautiful or nobly born. Either involuntary risk is an empty logical category, or it has to be a complaint against the particular social system which gives some people a harder life.

Chauncey Starr's examples are instructive. On voluntary risk: an urban dweller may move to the suburbs because of a lower crime rate and better schools, at the cost of more time spent traveling on highways and a higher probability of accidents. If, subsequently, the traffic density increases, he may decide that the penalties are too great and move back to the city.[1] On involuntary risk: "Probably the use of electricity provides the best example of the analysis of 'involuntary' activity. In this case the fatalities include those arising from electrocution, electrically caused fires, the operation of power plants, and the mining of the required fossil fuel."[2] The validity of these distinctions is not apparent. Starr, however, who defines involuntary risks as those "imposed by the society in which the individual lives," goes on to say that

"involuntary" activities differ in that the criteria and options are determined not by the individuals affected but by a controlling body. Such control may be in the hands of a government agency, a political entity, a leadership group, an assembly of authorities or "opinion-makers," or a combination of such bodies. Because of the complexity of large societies, only the control group is likely to be fully aware of all the criteria and options involved in their decision process.[3]

The key word is control: who is to control whom in regard to which aspects of life? Always there are unsuspected dangers. Always some inventions (asbestos, X rays), introduced to make something safer, turn out to be dangerous. Always dangers that are present are ignored. Since anything and everything one does might prove risky (perhaps when we know more, an apple a day will prove unhealthy or exercise debilitating or breast-feeding poisonous or showers enervating), we should ask why we face some unknown risks gladly and bristle at others. There is always government, which seeks to protect citizens against dangers with which they could not cope alone. Clearly, Chauncey Starr does not mean to justify unlimited government regulation. He suggests that it would significantly limit regulation if, drawing the line around involuntary risk, the individual were freely allowed to incur danger that threatens only himself. But there is practically nothing that the individual does in leisure time that does not affect his children or others who enter the home or even those who provide or share his sports. The climbing instructor has to risk his life rescuing foolish tyros stuck on the mountain, and the swimming instructor tries to save a would-be suicidal maniac. The fireman risks great danger when he tries to stem the damage from a drunkard falling asleep with a lighted cigarette in bed. Voluntary risks are likely to spread danger. Should the amateur climber, the suicidal swimmer, and the smoking drunk be prosecuted or forbidden by law to take risks?

Voluntary/involuntary is a movable boundary, capable of turning every constraint on choice into injustice. The distinction only stands up to criticism if one assumes a petrified social system with a fixed pattern of cultural values and fixed rules of accountability. Under this assumption, which is strictly internal to a particular culture at a particular point of time, one could allocate all known dangers on a standard set of principles between those that are individually chosen and therefore acceptable to the individual (like martyrdom and high-risk sport) and those that are involuntary, unjust, and therefore to be mitigated by law. In this form, a moral judgment of who is to be held accountable is enunciated by the boundary between voluntary and other risks. It assumes that the planet has to be just like this. It takes the constraints on choice unquestioningly as if they were given in nature, whereas they are given by cultural standards. If anyone wants to ask questions about how the boundary is drawn, risk by risk, the answers will lead in only one direction. Whatever was taken to be a natural boundary will be discovered to be a socially constructed one. Then political pressures can shift it back, ending with every choice counted as involuntary. All individuals could be treated as involuntary visitors on this planet, every conceivable damage they sustain could be attributable to unwished-for destructive agencies. If the pattern of values were to change in that direction, ultimately all the sick and unfortunate could be presented as involuntary inhabitants of their own bodies, totally withdrawn from any commitment to social life. All suicides and murderers would be owed redress by the institutions which drive them to their deed. All law would be compensatory law: individuals could be shown to have an unlimited right to be compensated for all losses, however incurred, if only the anger against institutions is comprehensive enough for risk questions to be all-inclusive.

IRREVERSIBLE RISKS

Suppose the changes we fear are involuntary because they are irreversible: once set in motion, they continue on inexorably until they cascade out of control. Irreversible changes are explosive and unstable, each deviation growing larger until the environment is so altered it can never return to its original state. Since such changes affect everyone, government is expected to regulate them in the interests of society.

Risk aversion is sometimes justified by the idea of irreversible damage because the smallest probability of a disaster from which there is no turning back overwhelms all other considerations. "If the extinction of mankind is evaluated at minus infinity," Jon Elster writes, "then it swamps all disasters of finite size. We must, of course, have some precise probability attached to this event: mere logical possibility is not sufficient. It does not matter, however, if this probability is extremely small, for an infinite number multiplied by any positive number remains infinite."[4] Immediately we are in the midst of terribly low probabilities of awfully terrible events. Infinitesimal amounts of strontium may accumulate in the body to kill off entire peoples. "The weakness of this argument," Elster continues, "is that it may turn out that most actions have such total disasters associated with them, as an extremely unlikely but still quantifiable probability. I believe, therefore, that one should be very cautious in arguing along these lines."[5] One should be cautious, but many are not because it is hard to resist the temptation to make a case against which there appears to be no reasonable reply.

Seeking to save a risk-averse inclination from the weakness of arguments extending tiny probabilities to infinity, Jon Elster holds that "the uncertainty argument for the principle of acting as if the worst will happen is much more solid."[6] Not knowing what is likely to happen — uncertainty signifies that one knows the kind of things that might happen but not the probability of their occurrence — Elster prefers to minimize the worst rather than maximize the best. He hopes to override weak or nonexistent probabilities with the certainty that there is no certain answer; for then it appears evident to him that, not knowing the damage we may do, we would be wise to play it safe. But would we? Is it our analysis of the evidence that leads us to play it safe or our desire to play it safe that leads us to this sort of analysis?

If uncertainty prevents or inhibits risk taking, when would risk taking be justified? Hardly ever. For it is precisely these issues that divide us: we are entitled to a different view just because knowledge is limited, alternatives imperfectly understood, and the consequences disputed. The very uncertainty that is here presented as the basis for avoiding risk in another context would be the good reason for taking risk; otherwise we would be unable to learn how to do better. Risk is also opportunity. If whether to risk and what kind of risk to take are the questions, they cannot be answered by saying that if we don't know, we shouldn't take any at all.

Elster suggests distinguishing among two types of irreversibility. He writes:

For this purpose it is useful to have the notion of a *frontier,* the value of some variable above which there are disastrous environmental or social effects. *Strong irreversibility* then obtains if (i) one can only know where the frontier is by hitting it, and (ii) it is impossible to back up from it when you hit it. *Weak irreversibility* obtains when condition (ii) is satisfied, but not condition (i). The first condition is a very strong uncertainty condition, saying that not only we are ignorant now about how far we can go, but that we will remain so until we have gone too far. "You never know what is enough unless you know what is more than enough" (Blake, "Proverbs of Hell").[7]

If there were agreement on the conditions of strong irreversibility—otherwise known as committing collective suicide—there would be no debate on risk.

If the future can clean it up, it's not irreversible; if the future can't, it is. The problem of irreversible action shades nicely into the argument over protection of future generations: should the future be sacrificed to the present or should the present generation itself accept sacrifices for its progeny? Put this way, the questions appear to admit of only one answer—sacrifice yourself, not the future.

Yet it should be understood that past generations, also acting on the belief that they were doing the future a favor, decided differently. As Noel Greis reminds us:

Historically, the courts had maintained a nearly unshakable faith in the ability of science to yield solutions to problems which would arise in the environment. In *Attorney-General* v. *Corp. of Kingston* (1865), the court stated that the plaintiff had to establish the existence of an actual and immediate nuisance, and not a case of "injury a hundred years hence when chemical contrivances might have been discovered for preventing the evil." The town of Kingston had been accused of creating a nuisance by pouring a large quantity of sewage into the Thames River. The court established that injury 100 years hence was not a sufficient basis for granting injunctive relief because science would probably have solved any problem which would have arisen.[8]

In the last century, prevailing opinion held that the future would have better solutions for its problems than the present generation could devise. They rejected "overconsuming safety" in the present in favor of allowing the future to decide for itself. But will there be a future if modern technology permits any fool or rogue to inflict irreversible damage?

Democracy depends on trust among citizens. If each believes the other about to do him in, coercion would replace cooperation. Should the United States, then, legislate for a universe of fools and rogues? The question is not so strange as it sounds, for if any action could result in irreversible damage, any actor could do irreparable harm.

In considering whether to prohibit biological research, such as on recombinant DNA, Dagfinn Follesdal comes up with a surprising conclusion:

> The answer seems to be no. The means of destruction which are already available for individuals with small resources are so disturbing that the risk will hardly be significantly greater if the research continues. This may seem amazing. Will not the many terrorists and mentally deranged persons existing in the world today become an ever greater threat with each new tool that can be used for destruction? Not necessarily. There is some reason to think that a person who is set on destruction and killing, and who already has means that enable him to do this, does not become significantly more dangerous if he gets additional, fairly similar means at his disposal. An example from another field may help to elucidate this. The number of suicides tends to increase rapidly when an area gets a new bridge from which it is tempting to jump. The number will probably not continue to increase if the area gets several such bridges. (On the contrary, it may even decline, since one is now faced with a choice and the original bridge loses some of its distinction and attractiveness.) The number may increase if in addition to bridges one also gets a tall building. Some find towers particularly fascinating, and not bridges. However, the number will probably not increase if one gets several tall buildings. Similarly, new biological means of destruction in addition to those we already have, will probably not increase the risk significantly. [9]

Worrying about what crazy people might do is worthwhile, but excessive worry would certainly be counterproductive. Those worrying about a plutonium economy are concerned that use of nuclear energy will, through efforts to prevent unauthorized use, result in severe restriction on liberty. And they may be right, which we would only know if terrorists tried to make their own atomic bomb. Along the same lines it could be argued that governmental health programs are paying out large sums from the public purse when individuals abuse themselves by smoking, drinking, and overeating. Might not government seek to regulate this abuse on the ground that individuals have no right to impose such high costs on the collectivity? Does this mean that Medicare and Medicaid should be abolished because they could lead to personal regimentation? As it is, highway users are indeed at the mercy of crazy drivers, and lunatics hijack our planes. We still do not make less use of road and air transport or cease to press for technical improvements, very much as if we did not regret these particular advances.

Once started talking about what a deranged person or a vicious government might do, we have a hard time finding a reasonable resting place. As Follesdal says:

If recombinant DNA research and possibly much other biological research should be prohibited, this would therefore not be because of the dangers of the research itself, which do not seem to be greater than the dangers of many other sorts of activity, as those of driving a car or of smoking. The reason would rather be the danger of misuse by mentally disturbed persons, terrorists and others. That the techniques are so simple and require little equipment, makes efficient control very difficult. The alternatives might become, on the one hand, a constant fear of a catastrophe which is very likely to come, and on the other hand, a society with so high a level of control that it would be even less acceptable, and especially since even in such a society one would not be safe against catastrophes.[10]

Here we have it; even if citizens were treated as rogues and idiots, they could not be guaranteed against irreversible damage.

If modern man faced innumerable choices among technologies with deadly irreversible effects, life would be like walking on eggs, for any misstep might be fatal to him or his successors. Therefore, those who claim to know what is, or might be irreversible would have the responsibility of controlling other people's behavior. Consider the connection between a governmental program to lessen the probability of irreversible damage and the means chosen to obtain this result. The instrument of policy usually constitutes a new agency or regulation requiring mechanisms of bureaucratic enforcement. The new rules create relationships that easily institutionalize themselves—government employees, affected interests, quasi-legal interpretations around which a body of lore, with its interpreters,

builds up. Is it more or less likely that the bureaucracies, with
their rules and regulations, will prove to be irreversible (so that
we won't be able to get rid of them)? Or is it possible that the
physical fears will prove to be unfounded? Involuntary risks are
bad enough, worse if they are irreversible, and even worse
when they are said to be invisible — imposed upon people who
are not aware of the dangers.

There must be substantial dangers to life and limb that are
hidden from us still, dangers that we have not found out about
yet, because we haven't bothered, because information is being
withheld, or because we do not think it worthwhile learning
about them. By accident or design, we may agree, not all
danger is out in the open.

It cannot be assumed, however, that living amid hidden
dangers is inherently undesirable. As Daniel Defoe has Robinson Crusoe say:

In my reflections upon the state of my case since I came on shore on
this island, I was comparing the happy posture of my affairs in the
first years of my habitation here, compar'd to the life of anxiety,
fear, and care which I had liv'd ever since I had seen the print of a
foot in the sand; not that I did not believe the savages had frequented
the island even all the while, and might have been several hundreds
of them at times on shore there; but I had never known it, and was
incapable of any apprehensions about it; my satisfaction was perfect,
though my danger was the same; and I was as happy in not knowing
my danger, as if I had never really been expos'd to it. This furnish'd
my thoughts with many very profitable reflections, and particularly
this one, how infinitely good that providence is, which has provided
in its government of mankind such narrow bounds to his sight and
knowledge of things; and though he walks in the midst of so many
thousand dangers, the sight of which, if discover'd to him, would distract his mind and sink his spirits, he is kept serene and calm, by having the events of things hid from his eyes, and knowing nothing of the
dangers which surround him.[11]

Evil intent cannot be ruled out. People do inflict harm on
one another directly, so there is no wonder they may do so indirectly by withholding information about probable dangers,

especially those not likely to manifest themselves until much later. Whether the motives are financial gain, political power, or personal envy, they can hardly be countenanced. Being hidden from the victims, the dangers are undertaken involuntarily and may even be irreversible. And who can give conclusive guarantees to the contrary?

At any one time, the history of scientific effort shows, there is evidence running counter to current theories. If scientific activity were to stop to check out all negative evidence, however, there would be no resources left to keep on working. Therefore it is generally understood that scientists wait until considerable evidence has accumulated before they are ready to challenge the conventional wisdom. Many negative results are attributable to faulty data, poor experiments, or other error. Is this delay an inexcusable flouting of scientific norms or is it a recognition that it is not possible to act on every negative finding?

Where does the path of virtue and good sense lie — in announcing every possible risk as soon as it arises, or in waiting until there is more conclusive evidence or safer alternatives? One side says "Do not start unless you're sure it's safe." The other side says, "Do not stop until you've got something better." Since it is not possible to say everything at once, or with equal emphasis, something has to be slighted. Some sort of risk has to be hidden. Is it better to hide the risks of action or of inaction?

Either way — by action or inaction, courting or avoiding dangers — risks may be deemed hidden, involuntary, and irreversible. If it is not the things you do, it may well be the things you don't do that defeat you. Is it not said that the road not taken may be the most important way? Isn't that road hidden in that one is never allowed to experience it? Might not what was missed be the only alternative to irreversible damage? It just might.

There are risk-taking people who believe that risk aversion is the main danger. They contend that the risk averse do not add up all the costs of all the safety programs, nor can they see the dangers averted by new technology or, in advance of experience, the benefits of economic growth. Would people voluntarily subject themselves to a lower standard of living and less safety? That is what the proponents of risk taking—nothing ventured, nothing gained—believe will follow from what they deem excessive concern with avoiding risks. To them, today's avoidance of tomorrow's risk is the greater danger. Can benefits as well as risks be hidden, irreversible, and involuntary?

There is, in fact, an institution whose proponents make the same sort of argument, only from a positive point of view. Advocates of this institution believe (often ardently) that the benefits it brings are hidden from view. These advantages are involuntary in that they are not intended; that is the beauty of it. Better still, these great and good results are most certainly irreversible; progress is assured. We refer, of course, to economic markets, which (in Mandeville's words) make private vices into public virtues, without anyone necessarily intending the result or being aware of its benefits. The one difference is that this time the hidden hand is a helping one.

Is it danger or safety that is hidden? How can one choose among these rival world views? Were it possible to calculate risk comprehensively and to agree on a relative ranking of dangers, doubt would be unnecessary. Risk assessment would replace choice of risk. By knowing the risks we face now and into the future and by assigning them relative rankings, technological choice could overtake social choice. But can we know?

II

Risks are Selected

It is easy to understand that before modern times natural dangers were used as threats in the work of mustering social consensus. We moderns are supposed to behave differently, especially because the same science and technology that make us modern also produce our risks and because advanced statistics enable us to calculate them. Before we decide that our own case is totally different, first let us try to understand how cultural theory explains the selection of dangers among people who are without the benefit of modern science.

The common view is that whereas past generations of humankind have been dominated by superstition, modern man is intellectually free. Fear of the supernatural does not screen our view of nature. For all other peoples before us, the idea of nature was a social and political creation; every disaster was freighted with meaning, every small misfortune pointed the finger of blame. For them, nature was heavily politicized. On this view it is our privilege to see nature as it really is, morally neutral. We owe our unique perspective partly to the development of modern science and partly to the whole package of other intellectual emancipations called modernization which comes with science. Modernization has taken the mystery and awe out of the universe, belittled the gods, or totally discredited them. The same disbelief in religion, which casts such doubt on heavenly intervention in human affairs, gives us the idea that "men, not gods, can rule the world, or that beyond there is nothing, just the void."[1]

If this is modernity, it would seem to follow that everything we can nowadays know about the risks we face ought to be direct knowledge: sometimes tentative, sometimes debated, our concern about risks should be about bare reality, as different from primitive, clouded perceptions as supernatural punishment is from the state penitentiary. But no! Try not to get into an argument about reality and illusion when talking about physical dangers. There is no need to adopt any relativist standpoint about what is really out there to make our point. We are only concerned with selection and priority among real dangers. On this subject we shall show that there is not much difference between modern times and ages past. They politicized nature by inventing mysterious connections between moral transgressions and natural disasters as well as by their selection among dangers. We moderns can do a lot of politicizing merely by our selection of dangers. Anyone who claims to know the right priority among dangers to be avoided and who also pretends that the priority has no basis in moral judgments is making two backward steps toward premodernism. The first is a claim to have a privileged, uncontested view on the nature of reality, which brooks no discussion, a claim which still flies counter to the work of science, as it did in the great historical disputes. If each theory is tentative, waiting to be replaced by a better one until it, too, gives way, no theory can be entirely privileged. The second retrograde step is to claim discernment among moral issues with the confidence of a physical scientist in the laboratory or to deny that prioritizing means choosing between political and moral consequences. Among the gifts of modernization is the belief that *ought* cannot be completely deduced from *what is*. To pretend that there are no moral judgments involved in recognizing which are the most threatening dangers is equivalent to the tribal consensus that attributes a punitive moral regard to the seasons and stars. To imply that no moral judgment is involved implies that the major dangers are so obvious that they hit the mind like a beam of light on the retina.

Our first argument is that modernization includes a burdensome responsibility either to refrain from politicizing nature or, if that is impossible, to recognize what is being said. Neither ordinance is easy to follow. Deep political bias slips into arguments that seem to be disinterested. It will be easier to recognize our own treatment of nature if we first try to understand what differences really divide our outlook on danger from that of premoderns.

There used to be an accepted difference between primitive ways of thought and our ways of thought. According to the philosopher Lévy-Bruhl, it was summed up in the primitive attitude toward danger and death.[2] He taught that after millennia of our human past in which dangers were said to be caused by witchcraft and taboo-breaking, our distinctive achievement was to invent the idea of natural death and actually believe in it. The concept of the accident rate and of normal chances of incurring disease belongs to the modern, scientific way of thinking. Faced by statistical averages there is no point in my asking why a particular illness should have struck me. If there are no deeper explanations available, the question about my own case appears pointless. Our curiosity is stopped by the doctor's certificate of death from natural causes.

By contrast, the primitives were lumped together by Lévy-Bruhl as people who recognize no such thing as natural causes. For them all sicknesses and misfortunes need explanation, especially fatalities. The primitives' questioning is not satisfied until a reason is given for why the illness or death struck a particular victim. In the primitive world view, according to Lévy-Bruhl, everything that seems abnormal is explained by the intervention of mysterious agencies called into existence by common fears and common perceptions, the mystic participations of the culture. For him, the defining feature of primitive mentality is to try to nail a cause for every misfortune; and the defining feature of modernity, to forbear to ask. Lévy-Bruhl's astonishment would be great if he were to behold us now, moderns using advanced technology and asking those famous primitive questions as if there were no such thing as natural death, no purely physical facts, no regular accident rates, no normal incidence of disease. We seem to have changed places —no, we have joined the primitives in refusing to quench our concern. They demand an autopsy for every death; the day that we do that, the essential difference between our mentality and theirs will be abolished.

Was the primitive, then, really modern?

Some do argue that our new attitudes toward risk are the result of technological advance. But this does not explain the shift. Technology has certainly changed our ideas about what is normal. Once we all understood the nature of statistical facts, we began to use them as ways of asking questions, instead of as answers. It might once have been enough to quiet the victims of road accidents or robbery to tell them the low probability of their having escaped so far: see how lucky you were not to have been hit before. But political change allows the concerned citizen to demand explanations for the rate of disasters. The questions that are asked are only limited by concern, not by technology. Technology plus statistics have enriched the idea of normal bad luck by adding the question of what ought to be normal. And here we come to an awkward pause. How do we decide what ought to be normal? Agreed that all babies born should live. Agreed that no woman should die in childbirth, that no one should starve. Should there never be any accidents at all? Should nobody ever die, or at what old age should death be normal?

One favorite explanation of our change of attitude is technological. Our present high standards of expectancy for health and life rest on the achievements of science. Low technology originally set the lower normal expectancies, but high technology has given us now the hope that any present level of bad things may be lowered. It is true that people in industrial countries are healthier and live longer because of modern technology. But this precisely focuses the paradox about primitive culture. How is it that premoderns all over the globe have long ago rejected the idea that we have only just come to challenge? Apparently, without benefit of science, they had already discarded the idea of normal, natural death.

It is true that for the first time in human history, we face problems posed by nuclear power. The more we recognize the novelty of our era, the more curious that we should turn around and join the primitive cultures whose views on death and misfortune we recently congratulated ourselves on having transcended. We cannot understand this paradox because our self-knowlege is sadly impoverished. We have made a barrier between ourselves and our past. We think ourselves so immeasurably superior that there is nothing that we can learn from our own origins and from other human cultures of our time. Some people whose state of technology does not warrant it can still believe that all risks are avoidable and strictly condemn each other for causing disasters. Our technology is new, but in its human effects our situation is not altogether new. People have believed before (and boasted) that their technology can deliver all mercies short of immortality. Admittedly, their faith in magic has been misplaced, but that has not prevented them from demanding commissions of inquiry into every accident and post-mortems for every death. At least concede that their trust in each other's power to do harm has brought them, without our technology, to a similar point. Not technology but something else in our society allows us to redraw the lines of moral responsibility. Principally, we have enlarged the scope for making someone pay for each misfortune we undergo.

One symptom of the times is the explosion in 1975 in the annual cost of insurance premiums which medical practitioners pay against the risk of being sued for malpractice. Insurers were catching up on the lag of premiums behind claims over the previous six years.[3] Looking behind the increased insurance claims, we find an increase in suits brought for malpractice; and looking behind again, we find that the American courts have been transforming traditional standards of medical negligence over a much longer period.

Between 1955 and 1960 the doctrine of informed consent in America grew up as an exception to the defense of consent which had been available to physicians charged with technical assault. In more recent years the courts have obliged a doctor to disclose to the patient in advance all possible side effects or other clinical risks associated with any medical procedure: failure to do so is now deemed negligence. In the British courts informed consent has no place in the law of medical malpractice, and the physician's duty of reasonable care would be legally discharged "by any physician who used his own best judgment on disclosure."[4] Furthermore, the American doctor is now accountable in law, not merely for his own technical negligence, but for the patient's actual physical condition.[5]

The American courts have also moved away from accepting as legitimate practice whatever is the prevailing practice within a substantial portion of the profession. A jury may now judge for itself the desirability of a particular medical treatment in a particular case. According to Richard Epstein, when a physician is sued by a patient the courts claim the final say on which medical procedure should have been adopted.[6] Medical attention has always been a risk for the patient. Now it is a big risk for the doctor as well. No wonder that the insurance companies increased their premiums in 1975 between two- and threefold.[7]

This is a change which has little to do with technology and much to do with institutionalized mistrust. There are societies with very primitive technologies which recognize similar claims of patients against their doctors. Among certain of the Athabascan peoples of Northern California the doctor has to accept full responsibility for manslaughter if his patient dies after he has refused to make a housecall.[8] It is not quite the system which Bernard Shaw used to recommend, that the doctor has to compensate the sick he fails to cure. Nor should we suppose that these people are overly credulous about the state of their medical science. The doctor gets away scot-free if he has met some acceptable norm of attentiveness and competence, whatever the resulting condition of his patient. It seems that he is only prosecuted if mutual trust is wanting. The Athabascan system of suing doctors is not isolated but part of their system of continual mutual prosecution for every kind of default or nuisance. In other industrial societies when the medical profession is able to lay down rules to circumscribe inquiry, malpractice suits are still as rare as they used to be in America.

To understand principles of liability, we have to uncover the kinds of social goals adopted and the strategies used for reaching them. For this we need cultural analysis that puts every concept of normality under scrutiny. Blameworthiness takes over at the point where the line of normality is drawn. Each culture rests upon its own ideas of what ought to be normal or natural. If a death is held to be normal, no one is blamed. Children's ailments are normal; no one gets blamed for their having teething troubles or chicken pox. Even infants' deaths are to be treated as normal in some societies and parents not allowed to grieve publicly. Special medical categories of normal suffering obviate the need for explanation or palliative; for example, children with rheumatic fever used to be told their aches were only natural growing pains. Normal accidents are treated as part of nature. Not every hunting expedition can be lucky. The farmer need not expect every crop to escape pests or drought. But of course the idea of normality changes with new knowledge.

Debates about new technology put into question the old perceptions of the natural and normal. The new technology produces new social responsibilities and provokes cultural reassessment. The line around normal dangers has to be revised to sharpen responsible behavior by refocusing blame.

A well-disposed reader, prepared to follow the comparison of moderns with primitives, would do well to start with the idea of pollution. We can sweep aside all conceptions of nature that rest on control by spiritual beings. Ghosts and goblins, spirits of trees or storms, ancestors, angels, even God—let us relegate all intelligent nonhumans to a place outside our inquiry. In establishing a base for comparing our politicizing of nature, the idea of pollution is a sound point of departure. Pollution, defilement, contagion, or impurity implies some harmful interference with natural processes. It assumes something about normality because it implies an abnormal intrusion of foreign elements, mixing, or destruction. It is used in two senses. There is a strict technical sense, as when we speak of river or air pollution, when the physical adulteration of an earlier state can be precisely measured. The technical sense rests upon a clear notion of the prepolluted condition. A river that flows over muddy ground may be always thick; but if that is taken as its natural state, it is not necessarily said to be polluted. The technical sense of pollution is not morally loaded but depends upon measures of change. The other sense of pollution is a contagious state, harmful, caused by outside intervention, but mysterious in its origins.[9] This nontechnical idea of pollution is particularly useful in political argument because it carries the idea of moral defect. Usually the dangerous impurity is attributed to moral transgression of one kind or another: it is presented as a penalty, plagues or famines descending to punish perjury, incest, adultery, or breach of ritual. Sometimes the evil effect is held to fall on the original perpetrator, or it may punish him the more by falling on his wife and children, or he may be seen as causing a community-wide threat. In what follows, the words *pollution beliefs* or *pollution ideas* refer to mysterious, nontechnical pollution.

Generally, pollution ideas are the product of an ongoing political debate about the ideal society. All mysterious pollutions are dangerous, but to focus on the physical danger and to deride the reasoning which attaches it to particular transgressions is to miss the lesson for ourselves. Usually we find that each danger from mysterious pollution is selected and constructed to give something like automatic judicial authority to the incidence of misfortune. Children die, there must have been adultery; cows die, food taboos must have been broken; the hunters come back empty handed, there must have been quarreling in the camp. Pollution beliefs trace causal chains from actions to disasters. Fifty years ago they provoked tomes about the defects of primitive reasoning, but now we observe how such ideas work in practice. They function to keep some categories of people apart so that others can be together. By preserving the physical categories, pollution beliefs uphold conceptual categories dividing the moral from the immoral and so sustain the vision of the good society. Our analytic task is to unwind the causal theories until they reveal who is being kept out and who is being kept in.

For studying beliefs in mysterious pollution, the anthropologist asks: what is being judged impure; then, who is accused of causing the impurity; and who are the victims? What are the processes for removing the stain, washing out or canceling the impurity? Asking this routine set of questions (What is the damage? Who did it? Who are the victims? How to purify?), we find the answers interlock. They define a category of victims who have some significant relation to the category of polluters — in other words, an internal social problem about guilt and innocence is stated in the pollution belief. Defilement is also a well-pointed metaphor of moral stain.

Nontechnical pollution works like a keep-out notice, a this-far-and-no-farther warning to some threatening transgressors. Many pollution fears are associated with sex. Ideas about sexual defilement uphold moral codes of chastity and fidelity by threatening default with automatic punishments. Any local set of beliefs about dangers following contact with sex tend to hang together as a whole. We may find that sexual incontinence spoils men's hunting, fishing, or fighting. We find also that a wife's adultery while the man is absent at war may cause him to receive a fatal arrow wound. Or we find that sexually active persons coming into close proximity with invalids or new babies endanger their life, or that the presence of an adulterer near the fire on which food is being cooked turns it to poison.

The list of sexual pollutions suggests that the culture will be prudish and inhibited. The fearsome list of restrictions, however, seems at odds with the joy of life and sex that obviously abounds when the whole context is known. We find that it is not sex that is dangerous but women who are too lively and seductive and men who are too susceptible to them to maintain the approved social separations. Look closer and it usually appears that it is women who are making each other conceal their bodily processes or teaching their daughters how to prevent female contact from spoiling men's activities or harming their own children. These will be societies in which women's social role is cast as betrayer. Delilah was a wife whose father and brothers were on the enemy side; her loyalty would necessarily be in doubt. Cast as Delilah, a woman is certain to be put under pressure to betray the man to whom she is linked and she may actually do so. Her friends insist on circumspection to protect her. It may seem extraordinary, but men often set up a social system in which their women are born to treason: then there is good reason for men to fear and mistrust womankind. In such a case, a theory of sexual defilement is a way of keeping women in check and relegating them to defined spheres. The women must know that it gives men a plausible excuse for punishing them harshly when the betrayal eventually occurs, so they try to be careful.

Cultural analysis shows us that ideas about pollution are not sufficiently explained by the physical dangers. These are real enough and there are plenty of them. Out of all the possible ill results, a certain selection of troubles is made particularly sensitive to a particular set of moral faults. The contaminations then work like constructed punishments. So-called fears of pollution, which seem to outsiders to be most implausible or unfocused, turn out to be systematic pressures to hold someone accountable, especially a wife to her husband or a worshipper to his shrine and priest.

These pollution beliefs are either part of an absolving process or part of a blaming process. We do not have to wonder how people come to believe in the mysterious connections. Plausibility is more important than belief. Plausibility depends on enough people wanting to believe in the theory, and this depends on enough people being committed to whatever moral principle it protects. The fact that the danger belief is an indirect way of laying blame at someone's door makes sure it will be invoked whether it is believed or not. We have to make

a great effort to realize that a community censors its own pollution beliefs and causation theories. Those which no one wants
to use can be easily discredited. Those which a large enough
category of people find it convenient to use will get acceptability. A child's colic makes a plausible occasion for a polygamous
husband to get confessions of infidelity from his wives, and the
wives themselves feel enough rivalry to believe in the danger.
The mother whose baby has died may not be allowed to express
her open resentment of her co-wife's flourishing children, but
it is a different matter if there is a credible theory linking adultery with causing infant deaths. She does more than relieve her
feelings by accusing the co-wife of promiscuity. Several categories of people, starting with her husband, will find it plausible to say that adultery has dangerous contaminating effects
and use the baby's death to uphold the vows of marriage.

Lévy-Bruhl and his contemporaries thought these beliefs a
sign of gullibility and mental confusion. But well-placed skepticism abounds and there is always a local scale of credibility.[10]
For example, in the South African Transvaal, the Lovedu
believe that their queen's anger mysteriously stops the rain for
the whole chiefdom.[11] At the next political level they believe
their district chief's ancestors inflict pests and crop and cattle
diseases, and at the level of the smallest social unit they believe
that the head of a family may be responsible for the sicknesses
that fall on individuals within the household: it would be quite
implausible that a mere commoner's transgression could spoil
the weather for the chiefdom, or that the queen's moods could
discriminate between her various subjects. For a total disaster,
responsibility is located at the top. The geographical and social
range of the natural disaster indicates the place in the political
hierarchy where the likely transgression has taken place (but it
is we and not they who call a drought a natural disaster).

When people believe in pollution of sex, around 25 percent
of their babies really do die in infancy and their mothers really
do face grave risks in childbirth and often do not survive. They
do not pretend to know the precise mechanism that makes sexual license fatal. Their selection of punishments are well

chosen to create the most worry and the most occasion for post-mortem head shaking and remorse. Pollution dangers are not imaginary dangers. The more the risks are real and grave, the better they qualify to play their quasi-judicial part in a system of mutual accountability.

Belief in sexual pollution seems very alien to a modern reader. First, science has changed our view of pathogenic organisms: neither adultery nor premarital sex is more likely than legitimate sexual intercourse to cause barrenness or difficulties in giving birth. Sexual pollution is a case in which the analogy between primitives and ourselves seems too strained to be serious. Second, our moral climate has changed. The weight of our social system does not rest on marriage and inheritance. To get a better understanding of how pollution beliefs are loaded with positive social concern, let us turn to a people who are not more worried about adultery than we ourselves but who are worried about the depletion of physical resources and by the encroachment of aliens in their territory and whose most cherished social values are their way of life, freedom, and friendship.

THE HIMA

The Hima are a cattle-herding people studied by the late Dr. Elam.[12] Their nomadic way of life has been easy in their fertile, well-watered land. However, they are convinced that women should be kept completely apart from cattle. The first of their pollution beliefs is that contamination by contact with women causes cattle to sicken and die. This belief entails vast consequences for their economy, as in effect it frees women from work. If ever there was a culture in which the women are unliberated sex objects, it is here. In the early morning the women dish up the simple breakfast, do a few household chores, and then they are free for bathing, beauty treatments, sleeping and making love. When the cattle come home in the late afternoon, there is a little more for them to do, in serving up the supper and doing the dishes. Otherwise their main duty is to be beautiful. The Hima idea of feminine beauty is rounded curves; to be beautiful, a woman must be fat. The fatter she is, the more lovers she has, who bring her extra milk so she stays beautiful. Though sometimes jealous, her husband must not be possessive about his sexual rights. He is expected to make her available for his own father and for his friends. Lending his wife is one way that he can attract other men to pool their herds with his and so make up a viable herding unit.

An important value for the Hima is the uncommitted free movement of men between the camps of friends. The camp is a fluid social unit. Each man has to worry lest he cannot keep enough friends close to him to make up an effective labor force. He has reason to worry if they are each seeking to set up independently and to rival each other in attracting a following. It would seem that the husband's control over his wife's sexuality is more important to him for making deals in the system of production than for her reproductive powers. They are convinced that the human population is going to explode and outstrip the cattle population. Their whole way of life would not be viable without a well-adjusted cattle-human ratio, for they subsist almost entirely on cattle products—meat of bulls and milk and butter of cows, augmented by millet beer bought from an agricultural people who live interspersed with them. In herding cultures it is unusual for any woman not to marry. (Dr. Elam was so interested in the spinster rate that he took a sample and found 3 percent of the older women had remained unmarried.)[13] But here the unmarried father's sister has a regular role in the marriage ceremonies where she cannot help seeming envious and bitter. The full, complicated arrangements of household structure would be long to relate. They make sense in the light of an intention to restrict human population. The old men do not take a second wife; they arrange for their sons to marry young and for themselves to have sexual access to their son's wives. Thus they reduce the number of independent households with child-bearing women. Girls are taught that their children will compete with calves for food.

Human reproduction is explicitly seen as a threat to cattle reproduction.

But is it true? We want to ask if the livestock is really at risk or are these fears groundless. Do the Hima live in a world of nonrenewable resources? The answer is that their country's lush pastures are superbly suited to cattle husbandry. What is primarily at risk is the Hima's traditional way of life. Their land is also ideal for agriculture. Their neighbors, the Iru farmers in their midst, desire the best valleys for cultivation. In other parts of Ankole, the Hima have become a minority, their old way of life has been eroded by the pressure of Iru population, and their young people have learned crafts and farming skills which their fathers utterly despised. No pejoratives are strong enough to describe the total contempt the Hima of Eastern Ankole feel for the Iru.

Here we come to the second major set of their pollution beliefs. Cows will die, they say, if agricultural produce is mixed in a person's stomach with milk. If a Hima eats plant food, he has to fast twelve hours and take a purge before drinking milk again, otherwise he will be held responsible for ailing cows. The belief justifies the rule that no Iru should be allowed to keep a cow; she simply would not survive the dangers of her Iru owner drinking milk and eating vegetables. Needless to say, intermarriage between the Hima and the farmers is repugnant and impossible. A farmer cannot even accept a cup of milk if he visits a cattle camp to trade. Yes, trade goes on; the farmers provide the millet beer, tobacco, pottery, and wooden utensils. But the social segregation is nonetheless effective because of the pollution belief.

You might say that the Hima are a people who believe they are living on a small planet. Their environmental resources are really being threatened by the encroaching Iru immigrants. Their own population is not increasing so fast as that of the Iru; the Hima do not want to enter into competitive procreation, already afraid their delicate ecological balance with cattle may be disturbed. They have seen the other Hima provinces give up the pastoral, nomadic life. Their theories of danger, so curious to us, have the usual triple compulsion: first, they keep

apart social categories which they want to keep apart; second,
they refer to real dangers, for cows do die and get lost and their
milk does dry up; third, there is the metaphorical message that
always reminds the men and the women that human reproduction must be kept down.

Pollution ideas cluster thickest where cherished values conflict. If a modern scientist were to enlighten a Hima friend
about his mistaken danger beliefs, the conversation might
go thus:

Sci: I have news for you; modern science proves that cattle
are not really in danger from contact with women or
vegetable foods.

Hi: Does modern science deny that cows get thin, milk dries
up, calves die, cattle disappear?

Sci: No, but modern science would expect you to give them
more care. You could easily enlarge the work force and
recruit women as workers. You could let women take
care of the calves and the milking and free the men for
herding duties.

Hi: We do not approve of women working, and the women
would not like it either. They would lose weight.

Sci: Then why not hire Iru to help out?

Hi: Heaven forbid! The Iru encroachment is our gravest
threat. They are digging up our pastures.

Sci: Well, take up arms and drive them out.

Hi: Then what would we do for tobacco?

Sci: You could try giving up smoking.

Hi: What would we do for beer?

Sci: You could try giving up alcohol.

Hi: Even if we gave up our simple pleasures, we could not
even work; Iru make our utensils.

Sci: Why not open Hima economy to agriculture and crafts
and be less dependent on cows and Iru? Life is not a
zero-sum game.

The Hima then explains that it is precisely the free nomadic
life that is at stake. He clearly believes the scientist is mad. The

scientist in this case goes away sadly, convinced that the Hima culture is doomed to extinction.

Our own theories about danger are apt to take on a similar, unrealistic tinge under outside inspection. What would a Hima scientist make of a recent Harris survey of American attitudes toward our environment?[14] In 1979 a sample of the general public gave a list of the current most pressing dangers: the first was crime and a close second was the increasing difficulty of getting quality education for children. Providing employment for minorities came way down near the bottom of the list of important tasks ahead. The imaginary Hima scientist might connect rising crime rates with rising unemployment, a connection which does not seem to have occurred to these respondents. Warming to his critical task, if he were to read on, the Hima would note a gap in the perception of air pollution between the general public and a sample of environmentalists asked the same questions. Do you feel, they were asked, that the air in your local community is clean enough? Sixty-eight percent of the general public answered yes; 80 percent of representatives of the environmental groups answered no. Inquiring about the discrepancy, the Hima scientist might be told that the general public is naturally more ignorant as well as less concerned than one who has made a specialized study of the subject. But if he were as sharp as Dr. Elam was about Hima cultural dilemmas, he would find that since the same questions were put to a similar sample a year before, the general public had shifted its view about the noxious effects of their local air. Compared to the 30 percent of the general public who thought the air in their local community was not clean enough in 1978, fewer in 1979 thought that the air was harmful for sick people, that it caused illness, restricted visibility and made you ill. On all of these points about danger from air pollution, more of the selected environmentalists disagreed. A plausible reason for the shift to a more relaxed attitude on the part of the laity could be that in the intervening year the air had really been cleaned up in all their different localities. But in that case, the Hima scientist would surely ask, why did the environmentalists not remark the difference? Of course sampling problems blur the answer.

Suppose the Hima investigator were to ask the four questions to be asked about pollution beliefs: What is the damage? Who did it? Who are the victims? How to purify? He would realize at once the seriousness of the charge on hearing that the damage affects everyone, living and unborn generations. This would tell him to look for top political responsibility, as in the case of the Rain Queen. Pressing home his questions about damage, asking perhaps whether it is apparent in death rates, he would discover that the American people have an average life expectancy of at least twenty years more than that of people in Northwestern Ankole, a much lower infant mortality rate, better nutrition, and lower morbidity rates. But that is unnatural, he would exclaim; it is natural to die between fifty and sixty; so why are you worried about the air and water? He would soon discover that the average life expectancy figures disguise the maldistribution of good health and health services. Then why not send the doctors out of the cities and suburbs and to the poor rural areas? He would be reminded that this is a free country and that doctors are not going to be compelled to work among the poor. Then why not extend the scope of public health? He would then learn that the major causes of death and disease are not from air and water but derive from the life style: between the ages of five and thirty-five, road accidents; between the ages of forty and seventy, smoking and dietary or alcohol excess. He would sympathize about the smoking and drinking and also conclude that people do not want this unnaturally long life or they would try harder for it. So he would suggest calling a halt to all new medical discoveries and health service improvements and using the health budget to bring everyone up to the natural span. But what is the natural span? Anyway, he would learn that the advance of technology gives hope of feeding the world. His questions would unleash a flood of guilt; the same environmental groups who are unhappy about the purity of the air at home are deeply concerned about hunger, disease, and want everywhere. Putting his finger right on the cultural dilemma, he would ask, "Wouldn't it be better to stop the new developments and share what you already have? Suppose we all aimed at a life expectancy of sixty-five for the whole world, no rich and poor, everything shared?" With this question, we would know the Hima scientist had gone mad. We could as soon stop worrying about each particular death at home as expect him to stop worrying about his women losing weight and his cows. We would hear ourselves explaining our defense needs, our limited resources, and our class and racial problems. He would find that living among us and on our boundaries are poor people, hard to employ, unsuitable to marry, uneducable, whose segregated residential areas are the breeding grounds of crime. He would think he recognized the Iru problem all over again. When he would learn that our poor are not another race, but our kinsmen, he would remember that complex pollution beliefs preserve the social categories. So he would refrain from asking why the rural poor cannot be given access to the seashore or why the poor city dwellers cannot be transported in bus loads to breathe the pure air of the mountains. From the way they are mentioned, he would guess the mountains are sacred.

It is easier to analyze pollution beliefs in a foreign culture. At home we are too close to the particular issues, too emotional. From grand aphorisms about irrational foreign beliefs, we fall into cynical bathos about how the environment is harnessed to ideology and self-interest. But pollution analysis is capable of doing better than that.

The Hima are clearly using their ideas about bovine nature to hold up a fragile social system. They are using nature in a rearguard action against change. Put that way, one would ask whom they are fighting and who are in favor of the forces of change. Presumably every little Hima boy and girl has to be convinced that the Iru are bad. The young men have to be kept away from farmer craftsmen who would like to employ them; girls have to be kept away from Iru men who would like to marry them. The effort which goes into keeping those beliefs alive is so successful that the Hima feel deep physical repulsion at the thought of desegregation. Yet it has occurred among Hima and Iru in other parts of Ankole. Just as cows do really die, so do Iru succeed in really transforming the Hima way of life. The threat is not at all idle.

The whole natural order is like an armory of weapons at hand for the war of political ideas. In the Hima case they have been selected and controlled by the reactionaries. In our case, protecting the natural order is not the social monopoly of radicals, but we realize that the critics of our society are using nature in the old primitive way: impurities in the physical world or chemical carcinogens in the body are directly traced to immoral forms of economic and political power. It is not only the natural environment that is polluted.

According to pollution theory the question of why the environmental movement should rise in strength now and not earlier has to be answered by examining the political context. Pollution ideas are an instrument of control. When the central establishment is strong, it holds the monopoly of explaining the natural order. Its explanations of misfortune make social outcasts carry the stigma of vice and disease. From the point of view of the central political establishment, the socially inferior are morally and physically contaminating, to be segregated and forcibly confined, punished if they try to break out. No one who subscribes to the center establishment view would suspect any possible difference between the current pollution beliefs and nature as she really is: nature is what the center establishment sees as natural. In the days of Western political dominance when Westerners went abroad, they saw other people's beliefs about nature as very strange. They wrote tomes on the mental aberrations of savages. Only a foreign word, *taboo,* would cover other peoples' pollution ideas and indicate a puzzling link between political morality and contamination in the environment. Taboo is foreign to ourselves because we can see the environment in its natural unpoliticized state.

But do we? Is it ever possible to see nature through neutral scientific lenses and laws? In the next chapter we ask whether we moderns can use science to give us an unpoliticized view of the environment. We will see that some of us disagree about scientific pronouncements. Scientists also disagree among themselves.

III

Scientists Disagree

In our modern world people are supposed to live and die subject to known, measurable natural forces, not subject to mysterious moral agencies. That mode of reasoning, indeed, is what makes modern man modern. Science wrought this change between us and nonmoderns. It is hardly true, however, that their universe is more unknown than ours. For anyone disposed to worry about the unknown, science has actually expanded the universe about which we cannot speak with confidence. In one direction, parsecs and megaparsecs enable people to consider huge magnitudes otherwise too difficult to manage, and in the other direction technological advance allows discussion of minute quantities, measured in parts per trillion. One might be entitled to assume that mankind can now be more informed about the smallest sources of danger as well as about the largest. But perception of parts per trillion introduces the double-edged thrust of science, generating new ignorance with new knowledge. The same ability to detect causes and connections or parts per trillion can leave more unexplained than was left by cruder measuring instruments.

Experts are used to disagreement. But they are not used to failing to understand why they disagree. So to find more evidence they take their analyses down to deeper levels. If no dangerous contaminant can be detected by an analysis that goes to the one hundred thousandth part, perhaps it may be found if we go down to the millionth part, or the trillionth? But expanding measurement only increases the area of ignorance. The frustration of scientists over disputes about technology is a characteristic feature of our time.

So much discussion is around that no one can take it all in at the same time. Thus we must content ourselves with a few illustrative episodes. The participants in discussion are annoyed and disturbed. They disagree and may well be disagreeable. A wide range of risk is suggested, serious enough to cause enormous harm, broad enough to encompass most things, precise enough to be worrying, vague enough to court challenge. Our techniques for finding new dangers have run ahead of our ability to discriminate among them. Sometimes the data are inconclusive; sometimes their meaning changes radically according to the state of theory.

Let us begin with "The Not-So-Clean Battle Over Cleaning the Nation's Drinking Water," as the *National Journal* calls it.

The American Water Works Association, which represents the water treatment profession, sent a letter to President Carter, accusing EPA of plotting "a nationwide scare campaign . . . to frighten the public into supporting its proposed regulations for control of organic contaminants in drinking water. . . . "

Officials of the federal agency see themselves in the forefront of a war to protect the public from the fallout of "the chemical revolution" that has bathed the environment over the past 20 or 30 years with literally thousands of new compounds that pose potential threats to living organisms.

Above all, they are convinced that these new, "synthetic" chemicals, cumulatively and in combination, are implicated in human cancers and genetic damage that may lead to birth defects far in the future. To support these conclusions, however, they must rely on indirect evidence — such as animal tests — or on human population studies with results that are "suggestive" but not conclusive.

In the absence of "hard" evidence of the degree of risk involved, water utilities — most of them quasi-governmental entities — are finding it difficult to justify the additional expenses that EPA's proposed regulations would entail.[1]

"Hard evidence" is needed because high costs are involved in this "increasingly bitter and emotional regulatory battle."[2]

To EPA, the nationwide capital cost, estimated at a mere $414 million plus $831 million for installing carbon filtration systems to reduce chemical contamination, seems quite modest. Compared to proposed air pollution regulations going above $24 billion, the cost of carbon filters amounts to only $1 to $2 per family per month, a cost which administrator Douglas M. Costle viewed as a reasonable insurance policy against the possibility of long-term ingestion of harmful chemicals. However, water utilities, now organized in the Coalition for Safe Drinking Water, have a higher projection of capital costs nationwide — $5.4 billion if many systems adopt the services and at least $1.87 billion if only a few use them. Moreover, they consider carbon filters at the proposed volume of operation as unproven technology. Why install costly equipment, the critics from the water utilities ask, for removing material that may not be in the water and, if it is, may not be dangerous?

Calling the proposed EPA regulations "internally inconsistent," Barry Bosworth, then Director of the Council on Wage and Price Stability, said that more lives could be saved at the same cost by imposing tighter standards on fewer cities, thereby taking advantage of economies of scale. This would amount to redistributing the risks, exposing some cities and saving some others. EPA replied that negotiating costs and benefits was inappropriate for agencies "dealing with the uncertainties of cancer causation."[3]

Observing that the dispute over drinking water "is identical to dozens of other disagreements," Dick Kirschten of the *National Journal* observes that this debate has been "exceptionally acrimonious" because professionals in the water field do not like to be seen as aiding and abetting the spread of cancer.[3] Further, since the water utilities sponsor the use of chlorine for cleaning water, it is worrisome for them to learn that chemicals called trihalomethanes (THMs), which result when water is chlorinated, might be among the main culprits.

After several chemical surveys, EPA concluded that there were over 700 organic chemicals in drinking water, with THMs the most numerous. Stemming from rainwater runoff, natural decomposition of matter, and industrial and municipal waste, these chemicals include chloroform — a frequently found THM compound — that had been said to cause cancer in laboratory animals. Though they found no hard evidence that twenty-two suspected cancer-causing compounds detected in water supplies actually cause cancer in humans, at least at the levels detected, EPA suggested a cautious approach including strict limitation of chloroform.

The water coalition would have none of it. It pointed out that 390 chemicals had been found in a single water sample, suggesting the other samples were relatively clean. It claimed that no causal relationship between chemicals in water and cancer in people had been shown. In any event, the coalition continued, the "overall incidence of cancer has decreased in the past 25 years" and this was especially true for cancers of the stomach, rectum, and esophagus, areas one would expect to be most affected if, indeed, there were any cancer risk from drinking water. The *National Journal* observes, however, that the coalition did not point out that cancers of the bladder are increasing.[4]

Apparently the evidence of human cancer won't show up for twenty to forty years. In the meantime, EPA says it has to rely on indirect evidence: "At congressional hearings the political figures won't answer if you ask them to set a limit on the amount that should be spent to save a human life. They take the stance that if there is a risk, then we should do what is necessary to minimize it." According to an EPA official,

It would be a gross error to look upon the proposed drinking water regulations as an isolated attack on the problem of organics. The contamination of the environment by synthetic chemical compounds is a fact of such overwhelming proportions that [it] must be dealt with on every possible front. No informed observer can believe that the tens of thousands of such compounds which are generated in so many ways in such staggering volumes, do not constitute a threat to the environment and the public health.[5]

This is no ordinary statement: If the public is exposed to a large-scale, hostile invasion of foreign bodies, almost any effort to repel it would be justified.

Before 1945, as Douglas Costle, the head of the Environmental Protection Administration, has pointed out, most chemicals came from plants. Since then, huge numbers of synthetic chemicals have been created, many that improve life but others that cause concern. (Of course, many chemicals do both.) Today there are around 4.5 million known chemicals with perhaps 45,000 in commercial use. "It takes a team of scientists," Costle informs us, "300 mice, 2 to 3 years, and about $300,000 to determine whether a single suspect chemical causes cancer."[6] Costle means these figures to show how large and important a task the nation faces in weeding out carcinogens from the oceans of chemicals. Total cost in money alone would be staggering. Manpower would be overwhelming. As Fischhoff, Slovic, and Lichtenstein observe,

If even a small fraction of these presented the legal and technical complexities engendered by saccharin or flammable sleepwear (not to mention nuclear power), it would take legions of analysts, lawyers, toxicologists, and regulators to handle the situation. If hazards are dealt with one at a time, many must be neglected. The instinctive response to this problem is to deal with problems in order of importance. Unfortunately, the information needed to establish priorities is not available; the collection of such data might itself swamp the system.[7]

Potential but untested carcinogens must, on this account, overwhelm whatever is known about safety. And this would be true even if current effort—say testing seventy chemicals a year—were to increase tenfold. If knowing the risks we face depends on testing thousands of chemicals, then we are unlikely ever to know.[8]

Water provides only one instance of the public being exposed to contaminants. Challenged to say how much exposure to a suspected carcinogen is safe, one agency, the Occupational Safety and Health Administration (OSHA), refused to budge beyond its position that the right level of exposure is the "lowest feasible level." Thresholds of dangerous exposure, even if they exist, differ from person to person so that it is impossible to identify an absolutely safe threshold for entire populations. If, as some research suggests, the risk of cancer increases when various carcinogenic substances act in concert, the agency believes it cannot set a threshold for any given substance.[9] Some scientists argue that the human body has evolved over eons, constantly immersed in such substances, so it is likely to be able to cope with natural levels of carcinogens even when they act in concert. If combinations of otherwise harmless substances cause cancer, and if almost anything can combine with something cancerous, other scientists offer evidence that the body is very vulnerable. Getting rid of environmental carcinogens will prove no easy task if the two terms — environment and carcinogen — prove virtually synonymous.

Tests for carcinogens have a "catch-22" quality: if substances appear carcinogenic, they are carcinogenic; but if they do not, they still might be. Since tests on animals are considered statistically significant only at the five percent confidence level, it is possible that chemicals showing no effect on animals will still induce cancers in humans at a lesser rate of contamination which, when the entire population is considered, means harm for lots of people. "Thus," a report in *Science* states, "a negative result with 100 animals tells us merely that less than 10,000 people might contract cancer if everyone in this country were exposed to the chemical at concentrations of 10 PPM [parts per million]."[10]

To find out what happens with low doses of carcinogens, 24,192 mice were subjected to seven different doses of a known carcinogen. So far the results seem to show that there is a threshold for bladder but not for liver tumors. But, as the reader might expect by now, the megamouse study itself has generated a certain amount of controversy. The basic difficulty is that the dose rates are so small and the observed incidences are close to error rates so that, for example, changing results in eleven out of 8,000 animals in one set of data might reverse the findings.

Two claims have led to vast public concern about cancer:

one is that death rates of cancer, responsible for about a quarter of all deaths, are rapidly on the increase; the other is that something like two-thirds of all cancers are environmentally caused. The first claim tells us there is something significant to worry about; the second, that we can do something significant about it by intervening in industry to alter the qualities of the physical environment that cause cancer. Let us trace the intertwined strands of these two arguments so as to understand better the concern about carcinogens.

Samuel S. Epstein, Professor of Occupational and Environmental Medicine, University of Illinois Medical Center, is a leading proponent of the claim that cancer death rates are on the increase, and that, therefore, increased governmental regulation of carcinogenic agents is essential. He writes:

Cancer is now the only major fatal disease whose incidence is on the rise. Standardized cancer death rates (i.e., adjusted for age and based on the total U.S. population) show an overall and progressive increase of about 11 percent from 1933 to 1970. This increase has been even more striking over the last decade, and cannot be accounted for by smoking or increased longevity. At today's death rates, the probability of a person born today getting cancer by the age of 85 is 27 percent (in contrast to about 20 percent for a person born in 1950).[11]

It is true that overall cancer rates for each age group have been increasing sharply in the last three decades. When one discounts lung cancer, however, which is closely associated with smoking, and when one corrects for the many more older people around today, Gio Batta Gori claims there is a slight decrease in the current cancer rate.[12] Philip Handler, former President of the National Academy of Sciences, assures us:

Indeed, the United States is not suffering an "epidemic of cancer," it is experiencing an "epidemic of life" — in that an ever greater fraction of the population survives to the advanced ages at which cancer has always been prevalent. The overall, age-corrected incidence of cancer has not been increasing; it has been declining slowly for some years.[13]

Handler insists that

Only a very tiny fraction of all current deaths due to cancer, in the
United States or elsewhere, could be due to man-made chemicals.
Moreover, only one or two percent of cancers can be traced to occupational exposure in such workplaces as coal mines, asbestos mines,
and factories; "pollutants" of all sorts may contribute to—rather
than cause—perhaps five percent of all cancers.[14]

Neither total cancer rates nor any specific kind of cancer
around the world, Handler states, is related to the use of
energy or the degree of industrialization. Where, then, do
most cancers come from? No one knows. Handler's hunches
differ from the school of thought that blames the man-made,
physical environment and he accordingly wants governmental
effort directed towards research.

It should be clear that man-made chemicals and radiation are, in
this sense, a relatively minor hazard that must not distract the scientific community from the task of understanding fundamental cancer
biology and addressing the difficult, complex problem of the influence of "life-style" factors on the incidence and tissue site distribution
of cancer.[15]

Since the question at issue is which kind of environment is
causing cancer—the natural environment or the man-made
physical environment—it is worth going to the eminent expert
who first claimed that two-thirds of all cancers were environmental.

When John Higginson, founding director of the World
Health Organization's International Agency for Research on
Cancer, compared the incidence of certain tumors among
blacks in Africa and America, he stated that two-thirds were
environmentally caused. As he later explained to an inter-
viewer from *Science,* Higginson's main aim was "to show that
most cancers were not due to genetic factors, and thus that
prevention was not impossible."[16]

He thought that the misinterpretation of his by-then-notorious statement was

due to a combination of reasons.... When I used the term environment in those days, I was considering the *total* environment, cultural as well as chemical. By cultural, I meant mode of life. When we ran that study of blacks in 1952, we started looking at their diets, how they lived, the number of children they had, the age of menopause, the age of menarche—all that was included in the term environment. I've checked it in every dictionary and every dictionary gives the same: Environment is what surrounds people and impinges on them. The air you breathe, the culture you live in, the agricultural habits of your community, the social cultural habits, the social pressures, the physical chemicals with which you come into contact, the diet and so on. A lot of confusion has arisen in later days because most people have not gone back to the early literature, but have used the word environment purely to mean chemicals.[17]

If a broad definition of environment is used, Higginson argues, changing one component may not do much good without understanding its effects on others and their effects on it.

Cancer of the colon is four times more prevalent in Copenhagen than in Helsinki. Both countries are well-off but have different diets. Should the Danes adopt the Finnish diets, Higginson asks? Well, Finns have a much higher rate of heart disease. Some people say fat intake influences breast and colon cancer. Yet rural Danes with higher fat intake have lower rates of breast cancer. No sense, then, in legislating lower fat unless you know why you are doing it. If Japanese men, and white and black American men differ one, two, and three times over in rates of cancer of the prostate, Higginson continues: "You look at that and there's no way you can possibly explain that on exposure to air pollution, diffuse dietary pollution, or anything like that. It is just ridiculous to try to do so."[18] Hence Higginson concludes, "We simply don't know enough at the present time in many areas to advise legislation or marked changes of life-style."[19]

Returning to the question of why his meaning of total physi-

cal and social environment had been interpreted as if environment equals chemical carcinogens, Higginson offers a political
explanation.

The ecological movement, I suspect, found the extreme view convenient because of the fear of cancer. If they could possibly make
people believe that cancer was going to result from pollution, this
would enable them to facilitate the clean-up of water, of the air, or
whatever it was. Now I'm all for cleaning up the air, and all for
cleaning up trout streams, and all for preventing Love Canals, but I
don't think we should use the wrong argument for doing it. To make
cancer the whipping boy for every environmental evil may prevent
effective action when it does matter, as with cigarettes.[20]

Environmentalists who object to Higginson's line of logic can
substitute a contrary one of their own: belief in industrial
causes of cancer is inconvenient to those who have a vested
interest in industry and who want to avoid regulation because
it reduces their profits and decreases their autonomy. Yet, this
line of logic continues, if man-made pollution causes harm to
other people, it is the proper role of government to protect
those who can not otherwise protect themselves. More is at
stake in the debate on the causes of cancer than mere hypotheses. Whole empires of industry and of government depend on
the answers.

In an article roundly condemning all concerned—industri-
alists and environmentalists—for bias and exaggeration, a
reader in cancer studies at the University of Oxford, Richard
Peto, attacks Samuel Epstein's *The Politics of Cancer*[21] for
misrepresentation.

To refute the common reaction that "anything given in large enough
doses will cause cancer in animals," Epstein's chief argument is to report that 0.01% saccharin has also been shown to be carcinogenic.
In support of this extraordinary claim, he presents in tabular form
the control and 0.01% data for selected cancers from certain multi-
group feeding experiments, leaving out the observations from those
same experiments which would have refuted it. This appears to be a
deliberate attempt to deceive the reader.[22]

Epstein denies misrepresentation, since "the caption of Table 6.4 clearly states that it is based on another table...." by someone else.[23] Epstein then goes on to accuse Peto of "misrepresentation," charging that

Peto associates himself with the insistence by the chemical industry and other lifestyle proponents that occupational exposures account for about 5% or "a very small proportion" of all cancers. This view is based on ascribing given percentages to known or alleged lifestyle factors, including smoking, fatty diet and sunlight, leaving a small unaccounted for residue to which occupational factors are arbitrarily assigned by exclusion. The authors of this simplistic hypothesis compensate for its tenuous basis by reliance on "educated estimates" and by making circular references to each other, often by "personal communication," as the responsible authority.[24]

The political significance of the debate comes out clearly in Epstein's parting words:

The role of lifestyle factors has been exaggerated, by those with an economic or intellectual investment in this theory, by largely excluding involuntary exposures to carcinogens and minimizing the role of occupational carcinogens. These considerations further illustrate the primary thesis of *The Politics of Cancer:* cancer is essentially a preventable disease which requires intervention and regulation at several levels, particularly the occupational and smoking. Failure to prevent cancer reflects major political and economic constraints which have hitherto been largely unrecognized or discounted.[25]

The thesis is that economic self-interest and intellectual investment serve to hide the truth about cancer; the existing economic and political system causes cancer because the system fails to take action against it.

Several doctors and scientists in the Three Mile Island area, where a nuclear accident occurred, claim that there have been excess infant deaths and hyperthyroidism due to the release of radiation. A professor of radiological physics, Dr. Ernest J. Sternglass, who has charged that the national decline in scores on Scholastic Aptitude Tests is due to fallout from nuclear tests, attributed a rise in infant deaths to the Three Mile Island accident. Federal scientists stationed at the scene said, however, that the professor had picked up "the wrong number," incorrectly provided by federal statisticians, substituting fetal for infant deaths. The right number of infant deaths, they say, shows no increase. Dealing with the claim that there were fourteen instead of three cases of hyperthyroidism, which impairs mental capacity, physical growth, and survival, the Federal Center for Disease Control in Atlanta investigated each one. Most defects happened before the accident, they found, or were hereditary. Though there were a larger number of infant deaths than in the past, proportionately there were also many more births. Besides, there were no appropriate statistics for past comparisons to tell what was abnormal. In general, for all of Pennsylvania, infant deaths were the same as in the area near the accident. The professor, federal scientists said, picked areas favorable to his case and ignored others unfavorable. These are the rival views:

Dr. Arthur Tamplin of the Natural Resources Defense Council, an outspoken critic of the nuclear industry, for which he used to work, said: "Dr. Sternglass never completes his studies. He doesn't go back several years to see what kinds of fluctuations might be expected, and he doesn't examine enough different areas to get meaningful data."

In an interview, Dr. Sternglass said: "It's certainly true that my studies are not complete. They need to be extended over a much longer period of time and more sophisticated statistical analyses should be used. But the data are suggestive of a potentially very serious problem. They fit a pattern that I've seen around other nuclear reactors and in fallout situations."

He said more studies should be done by scientists independent of the nuclear controversy, but added: "It may be 10 or 20 years before we see complete data from around all nuclear plants. How long do we want to wait before we start getting concerned?"[26]

Part of the problem of the nuclear industry is that nuclear power was a goal pursued with passion in the 1950s and 1960s. In the 1950s, the belief was that a new era of history was being ushered in, fueled by power "so cheap it wouldn't pay to meter it." Nuclear power was seen as so important that special institutional arrangements were established to further it. Nuclear power was treated by a special congressional committee, a joint committee of both houses, headed by an open advocate. The Atomic Energy Commission had both the powers of inspection and the duty of promotion, an arrangement which is contrary to common sense. Nuclear power received special government breaks, especially the government assumption of part of the costs of the industry (reprocessing of fuel, enrichment of uranium fuel). The government also took on the responsibility of paying for the costs of any catastrophic damage from power plants. It is not surprising that the fervor that went into nuclear development, and its formal institutional structure as an outright collaboration between big government and big business, helped to produce a fervent opposition, critical of big organizations. The Atomic Energy Commission for twenty-five years minimized the risks of nuclear power while the antinuclear movement, in dialectical reaction, maximized them.

When scientists debate among themselves issues involving risk, are they better able than others to separate scientific from political issues, to say what science says, or to apply it to public policy? They ought to be able to make the issues more manageable or the debate less acrimonious. Presumably they can quantify costs and benefits or agree on an estimate of the dangers. Insofar as the risks are physical, scientists might come closer to agreement either on what they know or what they do not know, for example, the hazards of low-dose exposures. But if the perception of risks is social, rooted in cultural bias, scientists should behave much the same as other mortals. Some scientific conclaves seem to be very like political contests, except that the participants are not limited by being held responsible for what they say.

As an instance of a conclave of scientists concerned with risk, we shall present an abbreviated account of a conference called by a distinguished anthropologist, the late Margaret Mead, in order to consider atmospheric risks, a conference held under circumstances designed to decrease bickering and increase scientific agreement. The title of the conference and the subsequent book — *The Atmosphere: Endangered and Endangering*[27] — suggests that the scientific editors, as Dr. Mead and Dr. William W. Kellogg are called on the title page, are worried, but it is by no means certain that most of the scientists present shared their views.

Why is there cause for concern? In her preface, Mead states that though human beings need protection, they have no automatic defense against their own environmental interventions "which have woven the previously dispersed and unconnected populations of the planet into a single, interconnected, mutually dependent and totally-at-hazard single group...."[28]

Why is it that normal defense mechanisms have broken down? Human life is made tolerable, Mead continues, by "an extraordinary ability to forget pain," but "this refusal to face the reality of natural disasters...has become a definite hindrance to survival."[29] Left to their own devices, in other words, human beings will take more risks than are good for them. But it is hard for scientists to get others to attend to future dangers if they cannot agree on what will be dangerous. No doubt Dr. Mead is correct when she says, "Only if natural scientists can develop ways of making their statements on the present state of danger credible to each other can we hope to make them credible (and understandable) to social scientists, politicians, and the citizenry."[30] On the basis of these proceedings, however, in which she had a chance to set the stage, the scientific chorus is still singing with discordant voices.

The illustrious participants divided into two factions, one stressing that the world ecosystem had worked for millions of years, accommodating large changes, so we are best off leaving it alone, and the others saying it was so complicated that even small changes could have great importance.

Much was said about the dangers inherent in even small changes in climate with their attendant effects on food production. But the need for intervention was hotly disputed by those who observed that the world had survived many prior abrupt changes, such as the "little ice age" between 1550 and 1850 in Europe. Since "we are only vaguely aware of the natural causes of climate change, and we have no adequate model of the climate system that we can use to make a good forecast for a year, a decade, or a century,"[31] intelligent intervention appears unfeasible.

According to Dr. James E. Lovelock,

Without in any way wishing to deny its [ozone's] importance to us as a species, to the planet as a whole it may be much less important than we think. We tend to forget that pollution is the way of life of many natural species and was so long before we appeared on the scene. Substances such as tetramethyl lead, dimethyl mercury, and trimethyl arsene have been dumped by anaerobic microflora into the oceans for hundreds of millions of years, their way of disposing of poisonous wastes of the anaerobic world. Perhaps the greatest air pollution the world has ever known was the emergence of oxygen itself; when this happened, whole sets of species must have been driven underground never to return to the surface, and others were destroyed. One has only to imagine a new marine system somehow able to produce chlorine by photosynthesis on the global scale and one has some idea of the trauma of the oxygen-poisoning incident when it happened.

Our capacity to pollute on a planetary scale seems rather trivial by comparison and the system does seem to be robust and capable of withstanding major perturbations. The doomsters' cliché "... and we'll destroy all life on earth" seems rather an exaggeration when applied to an affair such as the depletion of the ozone layer by a few percent.[32]

Scientists disagree on whether there are problems, what solution to propose, and if intervention will make things better or worse. One scientist thinks of Mother Nature as merely secreting a healthy amount of dirt and another thinks of her being forced to ingest lethal pollutants. No wonder the ordinary lay person has difficulty in following the argument, and no wonder the scientists have difficulty presenting themselves in public.

If the lack of agreement among scientists were due to absence of knowledge, as information increases, disputes would decrease. On the other hand, better measurement opens more possibilities, more research brings more ignorance to the light of day. The tendency toward confrontation instead of disputation may be due to the kind of questions asked, questions that do not permit of widely acceptable answers. If the questions are about how much risk is acceptable, social as well as scientific answers are required. When only low levels of risk are allowed, feasible limits depend not on what nature will withstand, but on what people will stand for.

Of course scientists themselves are people, not merely paid up members of the scientific community. Some scientists have been personally so impressed with the gravity of the issues that they have emerged from the laboratories to lend the authority of science to political lobbies. The result is what we have just described. They too have become polarized, inevitably, given the shortage of facts, between the risk takers and the risk averse. Dorothy Nelkin writes:

A striking feature of the new scientific activism is the public nature of its activities and the willingness of activists to engage in and, indeed, to abet political controversy. Disputes among scientists are normally resolved within the scientific community using well-established provisions of collegial review. However, recently, scientists appear willing to air grievances in a political forum — through the mass media, litigation, or appeals to citizens' groups or political representatives. Citizen participation is sought today for a different reason — as a means to increase the political accountability of science. While activists in the 1940s fought against political control over research, their recent counterparts — by calling public attention to conflicts of interest within the scientific community — seek to increase political control. Such actions have polarized the scientific community, as less radical scientists seek to maintain intact the principles of autonomy and self-regulation that were fought for by activists nearly 30 years ago.[33]

Where values are closely compatible and where most facts are agreed upon, attention can be turned to investigating the remaining problems. When values diverge sharply, as in the controversies over risk, fewer facts are certified and disagreements arise over what used to be taken for granted. In the midst of this severe dissension within the scientific community, efforts arise to save the essence of the activity by moving the demarcation line between scientific advice and political judgment. By observing where the demarcation line is set—more toward science or toward politics—the degree of dissensus may indirectly be ascertained.

Science writer John Herbers of the *New York Times* argues, "The scientific community itself is polarized and politicized, unable to reach a consensus on what constitutes an acceptable level of radiation when considered in the context of environmental hazards from other energy sources." According to Herbers, it is the "consensus of a range of scientists, government officials, activists and others interviewed recently, that because of rising public fears of radiation and the complexities, costs and uncertainties of nuclear energy, the political processes offer the best means of deciding the extent of the nation's long-range dependence on nuclear power and of safeguards against accidents."[34]

The President of the National Academy of Sciences, in an attempt to mediate between science and society, proposes a division between estimating risks, a proper scientific task, and judging what level of risk is acceptable for the nation, the traditional political task.

The *estimation* of risk is a scientific question—and, therefore, a legitimate activity of scientists in federal agencies, in universities and in the National Research Council. The *acceptability* of a given level of risk, however, is a political question, to be determined in the political arena.[35]

The moment there is disagreement or controversy, that is to say, when someone says a risk is unacceptable, the question *ipso facto* becomes political.

Observe the examples President Handler gives:

Do the alleged risks to public health and to ecosystems from the emissions of coal-fired electric power plants warrant the increase in the price of energy necessitated by scrubbers to reduce those emissions? . . .

Are the estimated risks of nuclear power plants too great to be acceptable; are they more or less acceptable than those associated with coal combustion? Is a very small probability of a large catastrophe more or less acceptable than a much larger probability, indeed, almost a guarantee of a small number of casualties annually?[36]

Obviously, in Handler's view, the disputed questions are political questions. Would he be saying this if he thought we could know the risks we face? No, in that case the President of the National Academy of Science would be arguing in favor of the use of science and scientists to solve scientific tasks.

We see how the argument must move from establishing facts to establishing acceptability, from correct answers to agreed conclusions. Inevitably we need ways of scaling the warnings and promises of science to the limited realm of political possibility. To accomplish this purpose, techniques of calculating costs and comparing probabilities have been developing over many centuries, from the simple bookkeeping of early chancelleries to full-blown risk assessment. Do the methods of risk assessment tell us what risks we face? Or does the choice of method imply a prior choice of the risks we have already chosen to face or to flee?

IV

Assessment is Biased

The political argument over technology is conducted between the heavily risk averse and the risk takers. The risk-averse side starts from the point that unbridled economic growth has hurt the natural environment and human life. The land has been despoiled, the seas polluted, and people diseased. The advantages of quantitative growth, the argument goes, have to be sacrificed to improve the quality of life. The other (risk-takers) side says that economic growth is good; it advises citizens not to lower standards of living by very much in order to reduce risk a little. It tries to convert the currency of discourse to a common denominator — lives saved or accidents prevented. Risk-assessment techniques are the expert answer to the question of how much wealth should be sacrificed for how much health. Experts try to show that many more lives could be saved or accidents prevented by far more efficient alternative uses of the same resources. The risk averse will have no part of this argument. They insist that human life is priceless and cannot be measured by vulgar money. They object that the whole exercise is immoral when life and nature seem to be bought and sold.

Risk assessment would be easier in a society so settled and so certain of its values that its processes for discovering the facts

and making political decisions would be judged fully adequate. That would be a trusting world, but it is not the one in
which we live. There is neither agreement over appropriate
methods to assess risks nor acceptance of the outcomes of public processes. Advanced techniques of risk assessment arrive in
the very scene in which they are least appropriate.

The problems at hand have subjective and objective facets.
Risk assessment needs to deal with each. When one wants to
know the temperature, one does not ask people but consults a
thermometer. When one wants to know how warm or cold people feel, one asks them directly because they are the experts on
their feelings. If one is interested in inferring the temperature
people prefer, given their situation, one can try to observe the
temperature into which they put themselves when they have a
choice. If one is interested in what temperatures are physically
tolerable, one can examine the ranges under which people
actually live. If one asks what temperatures are best for people
under different conditions, one calculates how much they lose
and gain under various alternatives. These alternative modes
of getting at subjective and objective assessments are also used
in the field of risk.[1]

The method of *revealed preference* is based on observation
of risks people actually take or accept. Instead of an actual calculation of costs and benefits, it is assumed that over a large
number of instances these have been internalized and an
appropriate balance struck. The method used depends on estimating the actual economic costs people pay versus the benefits they receive for various activities. Underlying assumptions,
as with all methods, are numerous. One assumption is that
what is true for the past will remain true for the future. Another assumption is that costs and benefits may be measured in
the economic marketplace. People have sufficient information
to make intelligent choices. Existing social and economic
arrangements are set as the standards for future choices.

The revealed-preference method reads existing social relations into its calculations backward. What people value is
based on patterns of action in the economy, which in turn are

based on the existing distribution of resources, which is implicitly pronounced good as the basis for choice. If whatever is, is right, this must be because the processes producing these choices are also appropriate.

The method of finding *expressed preferences* gets at the values of the public by asking them. Sometimes public opinion surveys are used; other times, the information comes from public hearings or interviews with smaller groups of citizens. There is no need to compare by converting values into dollars when opinions can be directly ascertained. Asking people what they would want, of course, suggests that this is different from what they are getting. It is assumed that people understand the questions, that they have enough information to give a considered answer, and that their answers are consistent one with another.

Instead of transferring the burden of decision to the citizenry, the *natural standards* method tries to transfer it, in a manner of speaking, to nature. Whatever levels of risk man and animals have lived with in the past are supposedly tolerable for the future. The trouble is that nature is a mirror reflecting whatever version of reality the looker wishes to see in it. Nature, let us say, is ample; it has enough diversity for everyone. If you want to forbid new things, just say that adding to background radiation or chemical wastes will disrupt the delicate balance of nature. If the bias is the other way, so that a justification is wanted for changing the environment, expound on nature's availability and the benevolent ways of mutation.

COST-BENEFIT

Cost-benefit or risk-utility analysis is an effort to compare risks by placing their costs and benefits on a common economic plane. Decisions are approved if there are more benefits than costs; if choices are to be ranked, the method is called cost effectiveness, the purpose being to pick the better of the best.

Though the difficulties with cost-benefit analysis are legion, it is useful for many purposes.[2] Indeed, we depend on calculated variances when we cross bridges or live in buildings. The trouble begins when we try to make calculations for purposes that are not strictly technical. Separating costs from benefits and calculating each as they shift from primary to secondary consequences is messy. The techniques inevitably tend to give undue prominence to values that can be calculated, not necessarily to the most significant.

Two assumptions underlie cost-benefit analysis: the major premise that economic markets are appropriate measures of what is valuable and the minor premise that no resource has intrinsic merit but that the mixture of resources is best that maximizes some objective. Thus the question of comparability among valued objects does not come up because it is supposed to have been solved by converting to the common denominator of economic value. Who can equate the preservation of the snail darter with the job of a Mississippi farm laborer, or the danger of eating too much salt with jogging injuries or with a nuclear meltdown?

Relating costs to benefits also incorporates assumptions about time, for costs are incurred immediately and benefits much later. How much are future benefits worth in today's costs? The value of life to the person involved may well be infinite. Valuing present versus future is a social judgment. Time discounting is done by interest rates. If technical grounds are used to decide whether to accept current rates charged to industry or a different social discount rate, the moral ingredients in the decision have been masked.

It is worthwhile observing that relating advantages to disadvantages is a part of all these four modes of risk assessment. The revealed-preference method assumes people or processes do this informally. Expressed preference elicits responses resulting in ranking of risks. Since introduction of artifacts into nature is bound to have good and bad effects on it (what will certain plants do for nutrients when they no longer receive so much sulphur from coal emissions?), balancing them off proceeds by a kind of cost-benefit analysis.

These four main modes of risk assessment clearly reflect the social values of the assessors. The revealed-preference method is based on internalizing economic market relationships; the cost-benefit method externalizes them. In either case the choice of method says the same thing in objective and subjective ways: that is, market measures are the best measures for all values. Those who prefer to use the natural-standards method or try to sound out expressed preferences are, by their choice of method, declaring that the highest values cannot be measured according to market prices. Each method is biased. For professional risk assessors this will seem a serious criticism, whereas the pretensions to objectivity are more worrying.

Risk analysis was developed as an objective tool for engineers and statesmen who needed more facts. They asked for objective facts. Objectivity means preventing subjective values from interfering with the analysis. Put the figures in, work out the probabilities, crank the handle, and the answers will come out. We have already noted the shapes of risk analysis in its various forms. There is the delusion that assigning probabilities is a value-free exercise. Far from being objective, the figures about probabilities that are put into the calculation reflect the assigner's confidence that the events are likely to occur. Since the risk analyst who feeds the machine its data is only human, he cannot focus on all prospects with an equally steady gaze. He is bound to select; and while he eliminates some other people's subjective bias, his own will be exaggerated 200 or 1000 times over by a computer that handles 200 or 1000 times more figures than a human head could analyze.

If the technology assessment process tries to guard against subjective values by multiplying the number of persons and interests allowed to contribute input to the analysis, then the problem of too much data produces a more severe concussion. The wider the consultation of points of view and the more probabilities that are fed in, the more the research design is reduced to a mishmash whose results bewilder those who take part in the process as much as the public and the legislators. No wonder everyone is left with his initial prejudices.

Something has gone badly wrong with the idea of objectivity. It is taken out of context and turned into an absolute value for all discourse. The rules that produce objectivity rule out someone's subjectivity. In a context of justice, an objective judgment is disinterested (but not necessarily right). In a context of social inquiry, an objective report is honest, free of personal bias (but not necessarily right). In a context of scientific inquiry, an objective statement is arrived at by standardized techniques; the inquiry can be replicated and under the same standardized conditions will reproduce the same answers. However objective the processes, the interpretation is not guaranteed right by objectivity in the research design. As well as objectivity, there have to be intelligence and experience in deciding which facts to include and which to ignore. Naked objectivity is not enough to make good sense. Yet from denoting facts established by the accepted objective processes, objective comes to mean some final truth about physical nature. Now, at the end of the twentieth century, we know that what is really out there is much more than our knowledge can grasp. There is so much still out there capable of being established by objective scientific inquiry. Science works wonderfully; it has organized some of the facts. For the sake of coherence, the intellectual energy that develops a theoretical scheme makes grand leaps over abysses when the facts are thin. At the same time, it relegates to the background yesterday's facts, which belong in yesterday's theories. The test for today is how well the theory works. But meanwhile, as no one knows better than the scientists, possible factual underpinnings for other theoretical schemes lie around unused.

When we look closely at how private individuals make choices, we will see that they choose not to be aware of every danger. The institutions in which they live screen some disasters from their ken. Their social environment sorts and clips the prospects before them. If they did not so edit their universe, they would be liable to the same stultification and freeze on resources as would afflict an imaginary government that might try to institute total protection and zero risk. Refusing to take all dangers into account is not behaving irrationally. According to our analysis the exercise of rational choice must include selection of focus, weighting of values, and editing of problems. But this editing process cannot be well done as a specialized exercise in thinking about risks. Specialized risk analysis impoverishes the statement of a human problem by taking it out of context. The notion of risk is an extraordinarily constructed idea, essentially decontextualized and desocialized. Thinking about how to choose between risks, subjective values must take priority. It is a travesty of rational thought to pretend that it is best to take value-free decisions in matters of life and death.

One salient difference between experts and the lay public is that the latter, when assessing risks, do not conceal their moral commitments but put them into the argument, explicitly and prominently.

> It was a risk but I took it because:
>   I couldn't refuse her dying wish;
>   I had promised my child;
>   I know what her family would say if I didn't try;
>   He would have done as much for me.

The private person does not isolate the risk elements to address them directly. When he consults, he tries to consult people who understand his situation: this is paramount in his choice of a lawyer or doctor. Only when desperate does he consult the unbiased, technically superior expert. Instead of submerging the risk elements in the larger pattern of social commitments, the medical or legal expert can speak to a narrow issue beyond which professional requirements forbid him to go. The ordinary individual admits that his loyalties and moral obligations are largely the matter at stake, but the risk expert claims to depoliticize an inherently political problem.

From recent research some very interesting things have been established about how people actually behave in the face of impending loss. Most people are not very good judges of probabilities. They hardly go out of their way to get information about dangers confronting them. In addition, they do not take note of information thrust vigorously upon them. They do not make the rational calculations that they are expected to make. They do not worry about remote probabilities of disaster. It seems to go completely counter to our impression (given in the opening chapter) that the vast majority of people in the Western Hemisphere are worried stiff about dangers from technology. In fact the vast majority seem not to be very alert to these or other dangers. Some would conclude that the vast majority are irrational and even that their lack of concern justifies a high degree of governmental constraint to stop people from ruining their lives.

Clear differences between the experts and the householder running his own life emerge in regions prone to devastation by natural hazards. The individual's unconcern presents a worrisome problem for public policy. Since federal funds are generally voted after the event to relieve the victims of large-scale disaster, it would help the public purse and the taxpayer if the individuals who wish to live in those areas would adequately insure themselves. What will count as adequate depends of course on who will pay the premiums or bear the losses if there is no insurance. The government agency considers the whole disaster-prone region; and if its experts predict a high chance of some household or other being hit at some not distant time, it will recognize a policy problem. Should there be compulsory insurance? Or subsidized insurance? Should people be stopped from living in the danger zones? Should insurance be required as a condition for granting home loans? The sticky problems arise when any one of these options is taken to the next stage. Compulsory insurance may succeed in reducing investment and keeping people out of the zone, but it is an extreme form of regulation. Subsidized insurance will presumably draw people to the danger zone and make it more densely populated

and so more exposed to tragedy. Then it is difficult to know
what rate of subsidy would be appropriate. The observant
householder has noticed that uninsured victims of disaster get
generous government grants to start their lives again. He notes
that victims who went to the expense of getting insurance receive only the sum for which they insured. (Such behavior
implies the private individual is a tough and wily customer and
not at all irrational.) Conceivably, the subsidy would have to
be very big to be attractive at all when postdisaster relief is
likely.

Each historic disaster poignantly illustrates the problems of
accountability we discussed above. It does not make much
sense to say that someone who has recently gone to live in a
flood plain or on a typhoon track is an involuntary victim of
the risk, unless there was nowhere else to go or no information
about the danger. So, far from being an involuntary and passive victim, the householder who goes to live in the danger zone
and does not insure often appears in the literature of insurance
as an exasperatingly willful free agent. But paradoxically,
individual decision makers seem to have a reputation for
choosing irrationally. Their odd behavior ought to suggest that
the accepted model of rational decision making should be
revised.

Usually, imperfect knowledge is invoked to explain the difference between their choices and those of expected-utility
theory. They cannot possibly have access to all the facts they
would need for a fully informed choice. If they understood
better and knew more, they would make the right choice. To
bridge the gap between the theoretical model of rational
choice and the actual, real-life choice, economists write costs
of searching for information into their equations. A cost that
everyone always judges to be too high to be incurred at all is,
however, a curiously artificial concept. It hardly makes sense
to speak of the costs of getting a commodity that no one wants.
And indeed this information is left around unused, even when
it is completely costless. It is extremely hard to get the average
householder to accept warning information, even when other

people are paid to convey it to him free of cost. Heavy investment in publicity with film, posters, and television talks has
been tried and found to make little difference in changing people's minds about spending on insurance. When information is
handed to him on a plate, the individual tends to look the
other way. Given his very negative attitude toward collecting
and sifting facts, his claims to rationality ought to be justified
by something more convincing than costs of getting unwanted
information.

An important research project on disaster insurance, led by
Howard Kunreuther, shows conclusively that individuals do
not conform to the theories experts follow when determining
what would be a rational choice.[3] According to the expected-
utility theory model of choosing in uncertainty, the rational
individual chooses the optimum course between probable
losses and gains: the optimal amount of insurance would be
determined by relating the cost of the insurance premium to
the chances of the disaster happening and to the magnitude of
the disaster. This process, of course, involves knowing the
amounts at stake. The Kunreuther research elicited from
householders in danger zones their estimates of probability.
Not surprisingly, the uninsured reported a much lower expectation of damage than the insured. In spite of advertising,
homeowners in the earthquake and flood danger zones often
did not know the cost of insurance and misestimated it. Of
those who actually bought insurance, 40 percent in the quake
sample and 30 percent in the flood sample estimated its cost so
high in relation to its potential benefits that if their guesses had
been right, they would not be maximizing expected utility by
buying insurance—yet they had done so. In light of their estimates of premiums and probabilities, 40 percent of homeowners in the flood sample and 20 percent in the quake sample
should have bought insurance, yet they did not.

This research illustrates the difference between revealed
preference, the actual costs people are ready to incur, and
expressed preference, what they say they prefer. Though what
they say does not seem to make sense of what they do, they are

not necessarily being irrational. The homeowners very likely have other risks to provide against. Their problems are far too complex to be settled according to classical utility maximization. In a famous article, Herbert Simon showed how to substitute the incredibly clever economic man of decision-making theory with a choosing organism of only limited knowledge and ability.[4] Suppose the choosing organism is not looking for the unique correct solution to a problem but only for a range of acceptable solutions within which to operate flexibly. This would be like the person selling a house who knows that an acceptable price will be anything over X thousand dollars; anything less will be unsatisfactory, and he will accept any offer above the mark. He sets a boundary of aspiration below which he does not consider the offer and a range above it in which his choosing is governed by his need to sell quickly, the number of offers he gets simultaneously, or many other considerations.

The idea of bounded rationality allows scope for social pressures to be systematically included in the decision-making analysis. The social environment imposes constraints upon choice and sets boundaries on the range of feasible alternatives. Insofar as social values get incorporated in the mind of a rational being, setting limits and giving direction to his desires, it is more accurate to think of the constraints of social institutions as internal to the chooser. As Simon has said,

> The givens in the situation of choice (that is the environment) and the behavior variables (that is the organism itself) are usually kept strictly apart, but we should be prepared to accept the possibility that what we call "the environment" may lie, in part, within the skin of the biological organism.... For example, the maximum speed at which an organism can move establishes a boundary on the set of its available behavior alternatives. Similarly limits on computational capacity may be important constraints entering into the definition of a rational choice under particular circumstances.[5]

Recent psychological research has reported on many simplifying procedures that people ordinarily make when faced with complex choices. In what they have called prospect theory, Daniel Kahneman and Amos Tversky have made subtle investigations into how humans choose under uncertainty.[6] They reveal editing procedures that discard from the calculation the components that figure in both alternatives of a choice. In such attempts to simplify by isolating a part of the problem, humans often fail to recognize a situation that, in its basic structure, is exactly the same as an earlier choice. For example, take this problem: In addition to what you own, you are given 1,000; then you are asked to choose between A (1,000, .50) and B (500). The next problem starts by doubling the initial bonus. In addition to whatever you own already, you are given 2,000. Now choose between C (-1,000, .50) and D (-500). The majority choose B in the first case and C in the second, demonstrating the reflection effect, which reverses the choices in negative prospects. But look closer and see that the last prospect has been obtained from the first by adding 1,000 to the initial bonus and subtracting from all outcomes. The subjects were evidently not looking at the final result, which would be the same in either B or D. If they really preferred a certain 1,500 outcome, they would not have chosen B and C. They disregarded the initial bonus altogether in deciding between the options. The conclusion that Kahneman and Tversky propose is that decisions are not focused upon final outcomes but upon incremental stages in complex processes. Stage by stage, what has gone before is treated as a boundary behind which one need not look for making the next decision; what lies two steps ahead is similarly treated as irrelevant. When two prospects have some elements in common, we ignore those shared components and concentrate on the distinguishing features.

This laboratory picture of rational choice as it may be actually practiced recalls the budget officer who is never expected to examine how the various budgetary items were set up in the first place but who gets promoted according to how well he can operate on the margins, for it is there that negotiation takes place.[7]

Individuals do tend to discard low probabilities, as we saw, but their attitudes in choosing between probable gains and probable losses are quite different. One of the oldest and most accepted generalizations in decision theory is that people are generally risk averse. They are also assumed to prefer certainty to uncertainty. Their simplifying is evidently different in face of risk of loss from what it is in face of probabilities of gain. Given the choice between a 90 percent chance of winning 3,000 and a 45 percent chance of winning 6,000, the majority go for the best probability and half the gain. When both probabilities are drastically reduced (to .001 percent and .002 percent) so that the chance has almost evaporated, the majority switch their choice to the largest gain. By what is called the reflection effect, the usual choices between sums and probabilities go into reverse when the sums concern prospects of losing. Think about it — you do the same: would you choose the certain loss of 3,000 or take some low probability of losing 6,000? If you are like everyone else, you would not choose the certain loss but hope that the probability would work out so that you do not lose anything at all. But in that case you have chosen a risk against a certainty. Against established theory, people are not risk averse for negative prospects, only for positive ones. We do not follow the simple rule that says to reduce uncertainty: when the prospect is negative, however enormous the possible loss, if its probability of occurring is low, we can generally push it out of the arena in which we are choosing. So we actually are creatures who habitually tolerate risks.

These simplifying procedures would be well adapted to biological organisms, which cannot possibly undertake enormously complex computations for every moment of the day. Humans turn out, after all, to be sensible creatures who have handed over the majority of their decisions to some kind of automatic pilot. The research that has followed on such insights has so far concentrated on the negotiating situation or on the formulation of problems. We now think it is time to incorporate some sociological dimensions into the description of simplifying procedures. Humans are not isolated individuals. Their sociality should be included in the analysis of how their minds work. In risk perception, humans act less as individuals and more as social beings who have internalized social pressures and delegated their decision-making processes to institutions. They manage as well as they do, without knowing the risks they face, by following social rules on what to ignore: institutions are their problem-simplifying devices.

When pressed to give an account of a decision, the departmental secretary will refer to the experts. The individual, too, when pressed, will make a show of objective consideration of the problem. In private life as much as in public, no one does well to admit having rushed blindly into big decisions. But in private life there is no place for the kind of cognitive surgery that the risk assessors do when they try to separate the problem from everything except the pure calculation of probabilities. The risk assessors offer an objective analysis. We know that it is not objective so long as they are dealing with uncertainties and operating on big guesses. They slide their personal bias into the calculations unobserved. The expert pretends to derive statements about what ought to be from statements about what is. The individual tends to start from ought and so does not subscribe to the ancient fallacy. If this were the difference between experts and individuals, good logic would be on the side of the latter. But the separation of ought from is cannot be clearly made. Ought depends on what is possible. The limits of the possible depend on what is known about the conditions of physical existence. And what is known is so small compared with what is not known that risk assessors are not the only ones who fill the gaps in knowledge with educated guesses. We shall see in the next chapters that the kinds of guesses about natural existence depend very largely on the kinds of moral education of the people doing the guessing. This of course applies as much to the expert risk assessors as to the public.

Everyone, expert and layman alike, is biased. No one has a social theory above the battle. Knowledge of danger is necessarily partial and limited: judgments of risk and safety must be selected as much on the basis of what is valued as on the basis of what is known. Thus the difference diminishes between modern mankind and its predecessors. Science and risk assessment cannot tell us what we need to know about threats of danger since they explicitly try to exclude moral ideas about the good life. Where responsibility starts, they stop.

Individuals who unload the decision-making process onto institutional processes are not washing their hands of responsibility. The responsible action is to have built good monitoring devices so that one's own principles will be defended by friends and neighbors. Family life and work life focus and restrict the individual vision. Careful to avoid disgrace and conscious of the need of support, the social being is a sensitive scanner of safety signs in a universe of critical fellow humans who share his commitments. It seems that rational human behavior does not use elaborate calculation for making crisis decisions, nor does it separate out risks one by one or two by two. Rather it focuses on the infrastructure of everyday comportment, setting up the conditions for surviving crises by building flexible, feasible aims into a way of life. One can well say that individual decisions are less complicated than national decisions, but the methods of simplifying are still sound. Serious risk analysis should also focus on the institutional framework of decision making. The real choices that lead most directly to dangerous decisions are choices about social institutions. This is what the risk-averse voice has been saying all along. The upshot of our whole argument is that one should listen to the plaint against institutions. Instead of being distracted by dubious calculations, we should focus our analysis just there, on what is wrong with the state of society.

Technology assessment was originally introduced to place risk analysis in its social context. It always has a column in its calculations called "State of Society Assumptions," which are supposed to indicate what is going to be acceptable. For lack of knowing what assumptions about the state of society are relevant, the column only carries trivial information or hilarious inconsequentialities. Our analysis is intended to provide something more enlightening about the state of society. We believe that people's first and fundamental choices are personal, moral, and political; the intellectual arguments justify what has been decided: first the good society, the good life, and a place in it; explanations later. If we agreed on what polity we desired, we could consider what risks would be worth facing for establishing it.

V

The Center is Complacent

The computer can do it, but "people may have great difficulty making decisions about gambles when they are forced to resolve conflicts generated by the possibility of experiencing both gains and losses, and uncertain ones at that."[1] From this, the next step is to remedy human limitations as one would improve the design of a computer program. Improve the labeling on poisons, smarten the packaging of information about risks, then all that is required for correct perception is to rev up the reasoning process. "Decisions about risk require sophisticated reasoning on behalf of both experts and the public. Needed are an appreciation of the probabilistic nature of the world and the ability to think intelligently about rare (but consequential) events."[2]

A vast and sophisticated literature on risk perception[3] assumes that the right probabilistic calculations would be enough to settle questions about worthwhile risks. But we demur. First, probabilism is partly a feature of the world and partly a feature of a certain kind of thinking about the world that works well. Second, probabilities are calculated from data and cannot be helpful to a decision if sufficient relevant data have not been included. Third, choice between important issues has moral implications. Choice is about the future.

Choice requires selection, and selection demands judgment not only about what is but what ought to be in the future. Somehow, somewhere, a moral judgment has to be dredged up from or imposed upon all the data. Adding more data will not always make the choice easier. Some parts of the question have to be put into the shade so as to highlight a more manageable choice between losses and gains.[4] If simplifying devices are used when making hypothetical choices in the psychological laboratory, how much more simplification occurs in the hustle and bustle of the real world.

To understand risk perception we should ask what makes a danger seem highly improbable when the psychologist is not providing percentages on the probabilities. We should ask how gains are ranked when there is no clear money standard on which to compare them. The current theories of risk perception steer badly between overintellectualizing the decision process and overemphasizing irrational impediments. It is as if the individual would shun them forthwith if he could only perceive the dangers to health and safety that the expert knows. This is to intellectualize the uses of knowledge beyond all reason. The satisfactions in smoking and drinking and driving are not private pleasures. Even if they were, habits would still be hard to change because they are locked into life styles. But most habits, good and bad, are social, rooted in community life. One does not always feel free to admonish friends to change their work and leisure patterns or even to utter the silent reproach of deviation, and to drop out of the shared occasions is asking too much. It is quite enough of an effort to meet the criticism of fellows by coming up to their standards; getting them to adopt new ones decreed by the health authorities is quite another thing. This is the point: anyone who lives in a community is monitored; the more close-knit, the more mutual monitoring. The child cannot read, the dog barks at night, the wife looks ill, the house is a mess — community is interested in these failings, advice flows, and names of doctors, teachers, and other services are proffered. Community life criticizes meanness, lateness, and prodigality according to its standard. Since such monitoring constitutes the social bond, sudden accidents and lingering disease are always occasions of criticism. In a tight community a man has his work cut out to meet the neighbors' standards. This is where he gets the health education that he cannot ignore. When the community bond is weaker, he can relax. He can pick and choose among his friends; but unless he is totally isolated, his acquaintances to whom he goes for solace are his sources of risk warning. A real-life risk portfolio is not a selection made by private ratiocination. In real life the social process slides the decision making and the prior editing of choices onto social institutions. Shared values do more than weight the calculation of risks. They work on the estimates of probabilities as well as on the perceived magnitudes of loss.

Nothing influences the estimate of probabilities more than the sense of future time. Most people conceive the future as a straight extension of the present, but there are large variations. An economist, reflecting on differences in the perception of the long term, says;

Even an individual, short as the span of his life may be . . . considers the long term trend of his active life, prepares for it and allows for it. . . . A similar argument applies with greater force regarding individuals in their capacity as members of business enterprises or of other institutional units. . . . In theory, and often in actual practice, these non-family institutions act as if endowed with eternal life. Their time-horizon, therefore, can be and often is much wider than that of individuals acting as members of family units.[5]

Oscar Lewis maintained that the condition of poverty foreshortens the future. The very poor, not knowing where the next meal will come from, get the habit of living so entirely in the present that they do not imagine the future at all.[6]

Comparison of risk perception should allow for social influences on perceptions of time. The official view of how to assess a slice of the future starts from the experience of time measured by clocks and calendars and by projections upon these measures. Actually calendars function to carry social information in the divisions of the weeks and years, but they have been specially constructed to be free of social bias in the measurement of time as such. Though they are objective, abstract, and independent measures, no one who uses them pays simultaneous and equal attention to the whole period potentially marked out. Attention focuses here and relaxes elsewhere; time drags or time speeds by. How people perceive the temporal aspects of risk depends on the span of their attention.

Time is a concept inextricably bound up with anticipation and memory. Only other people can make good the promises stored in the future. The possibilities of looking forward and looking backward are limited by social conditions. There are individual differences, but it is safe to say that an individual's expectation of the future must be influenced by an assessment of how likely the current set of social institutions is to endure. An individual can expect to get future rewards only if he can reasonably suppose that those in his debt will be in a position (and somehow obliged) to repay him. If he has to adapt to uncertainty, he will be wise to cancel those expectations. If a whole society starts to adapt to general uncertainty, its future will be stripped of anticipated returns. Each will be wise to call in his debts now and refuse to lend. A long-time perspective in which rich rewards pile up for a respected old age depends on confidence in other people. When we find people living together with graduated expectations for the long term, we can fairly well surmise what they must have been doing to keep that confidence in the future alive and green. They must have posted lookouts to warn them of defaulters. They must have been quick to recognize a threat of separation as a threat to their own future. If groups of young people are allowed to splinter off, who will be left to deliver the pension scheme? To maintain a rosy expectation of the long term they must exert continual vigilance in justifying the present system, with its delayed satisfactions and whatever inequalities are part of it. If the opposition claims that risks are hidden, the establishment counters that benefits are invisible but real, as in Adam Smith's "hidden hand" of the economic market. They can hardly resist calling in the terrors of nature and the vulnerable balance of the environment to strengthen the claims of mutual indebtedness between the generations.

A particular selection of dangers will characterize the society that constructs itself toward long-term goals. Such a society will emphasize the value of traditions and link them with nature so intimately that a drought or epidemic will plausibly be traced to disrespect of the past. The social past and social future are like a balance: if one is long, the other must be just as long; if the future is to be heavy, the past must be equally so. This is not a mystical announcement but a straight sociological inference. The vista of the future is made of claims of one generation against the next: from one standpoint the claims stretch forward; from the other they stretch back. The converse holds: a future that only has a short term is unmortgaged; its past has not been allowed to stake forward claims. Living in the present means inventing cutout mechanisms which prevent that future from being cluttered with a load of obligations.

The perceiving subjects who do the risk-perception tests are the same persons who may have decided to maintain communal confidence in a long-term future or to close the future down around their mutual mistrust and uncertainties, but this bias is concealed by the form of the tests. Everyone committed to a form of social life is committed to an appropriate structuring of time. Every form of social life, if it endures at all, digs its own channels of memory and its own shapes of amnesic spaces, just as important as memory, for allowing that social type to persist. Each form of society shuts out perception of some dangers and highlights others. If attitudes toward time are so different, the wonder is not that people favor different estimates of long-term probabilities but that they ever agree at all. If the differences were random, there would be no point in following up this line of thought. But deep differences in attitudes toward risk derive from institutional life—and these can be traced.

Apart from estimating the appropriate time scale for a problem of choice, even the very size of a problem is differently estimated according to the cultural bias that is part and parcel of institutions for organizing action. People who have recently been through a bad experience, such as an earthquake or a flood, are more able to imagine it happening to themselves again. The more distant the news of a disaster, the more difficult to get the imagination to respond; the more dramatic a story of loss, the easier to remember it. Some institutions keep the story of past trials alive, while others consign bad memories to oblivion and cherish only good ones. In assigning magnitudes to a possible disaster, everything depends on which bits of information are included and which ignored.

General social orientations — say a zero-sum or an expanding-sum view of wealth, short or long time-horizons, concentration on losses or gains — guide selection of risks. Overall goals provide the selective principles, and there is reason to believe that the latent goals of an organization are more influential than those more openly acknowledged. While a risk expert may be told to work out the costs of achieving a certain objective, other, more powerful motivations may lie behind the mandate, never spoken because taken utterly for granted, built into the fabric of the institution. Trade-offs have to be conceived in the relatively short term. The longer the term ahead, the more uncertainties creep into the sums. But the long-range goals that have to do with keeping a certain kind of social system in being are generally the most potent for stirring the emotions. Suppose one kind of institution encourages everyone to adopt the limited-good, zero-sum mentality.[7] This is an outlook which assumes that no one benefits except at the expense of his fellows; every gain for one is another's loss. This mentality easily follows the reasoning of the trade-offs, but it is likely to take the results of cost-benefit analysis much more literally and seriously than the other mentality that believes in an expanding economic universe. Some institutions keep expansion as a cherished, hidden goal; and since by expansion they can hope to defeat the most gloomy theorems, people living in such institutions would not take the trade-off calculations so seriously. Here, then, are some examples of how cultural pressures embodied in institutions supply the editing processes that affect rational choice. Probabilities and values are not so easy to keep apart. The same influences that edit (or bias) probabilities in certain ways will also edit values.

Another difference in attitudes toward risk derives from confidence in the current procedures for assessment. Some forms of institutional life encourage the idea that all formal procedures are prone to error because they are too mechanical. Mannheim found this bias justifying government by an aristocratic elite. The *je ne sais quoi* element in politics is an unorganized and incalculable realm, which would only be learned over numerous generations of experience and never codified.[8] There are other similar sources of contempt for the set procedures and rational deductions of bureaucrats and business, sources that have nothing to do with an aristocratic tradition. Risk analysts can calculate till they are blue in the face; their calculations will never prevail against this bias.

When institutions present choices to their members, they may present either the loss or the gain as the dominant element, according to the kind of institution. Some institutional forms create problems that can best be solved by expansion. The overwhelming advantages of expansion may be so dominant in everyone's minds that the gains would come to the fore in any presentation of a choice about a territorial grab, and the chance of losses would fade. Or, again, people who have general confidence in the counteractive and anticipatory powers of their institutions may be disposed to estimate probabilities of loss differently from people who mistrust their institutions. These three factors, the editing out of losses, the confidence in assessment procedures, and the feeling for future time, affect both estimated probabilities and magnitudes.

Cultural analysis does not ask about people's private beliefs. It asks what theories about the world emerge as guiding principles in a particular form of society. To apply this kind of analysis, we assume that a social form is always precarious because members of civil society try to alter it. Consequently there is always a debate about culture, about beliefs and values. If a social system stays stable, say over twenty or fifty years, it is because the upholders of the present constitution were able to win the debate thus far and to muster public agreement to the supporting beliefs and values.

Western social thought habitually reverts to a typology of two, bureaucracy contrasted with the market. We know the organizational limits of these types, we know their style of decision making, their hidden assumptions and manifest priorities. An individual who passes his life exclusively in one or another such social environment internalizes its values and bears its marks on his personality. It follows that he also gets a distinctive attitude toward risks. Here we shall extend the range of the typology. We include bureaucratic behavior with the behavior that characterizes all large organizations, under the head of hierarchy. This restores the word to its full sense. The author of *Homo Hierarchicus* says that the characteristic of hierarchy is that all parts are oriented towards the whole, so that formally "a hierarchical relation is a relation between larger and smaller or more precisely between *that which encompasses* and that which is encompassed."[9] Under the head of hierarchy, including churches, industrial corporations, and political hierarchies, we include the bureaucratic behavior that characterizes all large organizations. Contrasted with hierarchy, we use *individualism* for the behavior that includes market and sustained private profit-seeking of all kinds. Each type creates a social environment in which distinctive strategies have to be adopted if both the individual member and the form of organization is to survive.

If a hierarchical collective (or hierarchy, as we shall say in what follows) has successfully endured over time and spread its area of control, it will have managed to suppress internal rivalries so that mighty individuals do not tear it apart. Its success depends on not allowing one member's personal glory to be distinguished from the collective honor. Likewise and in consequence, no one member can be forced to take blame. Collectivizing responsibility is done by making roles anonymous. Decision making should ideally be so collectivized that no one is seen to decide. If all operate on fixed instructions, everyone executes and no one decides policies. Mannheim said that bureaucracy is a type of organization that turns all policy issues into administrative problems. It eschews politics and closes its eyes to the scenes in which laws have their genesis, the secret negotiations and public debates of political strife.[10] A successful bureaucratic hierarchy includes many interacting subunits which would be tempted to break away if there were no advantages in staying within the fold.[11] Consequently the strategy emerges of compromise, of not pressing problems to the point of defining a single overriding objective, and of creating a complex and obscure tradition in which each subunit can find its place. To keep the subunits from fearing for their sectional interests, the hierarchy avoids adopting a single overriding goal.

As Dumont has remarked, a hierarchy is more tolerant than a society of equal individuals. So it consistently avoids internal as well as external politics. These apolitical people are so little used to harkening to political sounds that they cannot distinguish between temporary, local perturbation and a major upheaval. According to Mannheim they regard revolution "as an untoward event within an otherwise ordered system and not as a living expression of fundamental social forces on which the existence, the preservation and the development of society depends. The juristic administrative mentality constructs only closed static systems of thought, and is always faced with the paradoxical task of having to incorporate into its system new laws, which arise out of the unsystematized interaction of living forces as if they were only a further elaboration of the original system."[12] If such an organization is to endure, the demands of internal coalition will be a prior concern of members; no one section or person will be able to dominate the organization for long, but they can impose constraints upon one another. Individuals are constantly made aware of the limitations on their own possible achievements. Realism damps idealism. It follows that the most passionately interesting problems for members have to do with the relative standing of the subunits and their scope for territorial gains. Graham Allison gives a lively account of the effect of organization processes on decision making when he reviews the accounts of United States Government perceptions of risk on the occasion of the Pearl Harbor attack and the Cuban Missile Crisis. "When a breakthrough cracked the Japanese codes, the question in the Navy was less 'What do these messages mean?' than 'Who would perform the task of serious evaluation of the enemy intentions?' This issue pitted the office of Naval Intelligence against the War Plans Division." Though it lacked Japanese linguists and specialists, the latter, the more powerful agency, won the right to "interpret and evaluate all information concerning possible hostile nations from whatever source received."[13]

When people who are trying to keep a hierarchy in being have settled to do it by avoiding turbulent social processes and by avoiding choice among ultimate goals or anything that resists codification or provokes major disagreements, they must steer clear of the deeper intellectual problems. The numerous attempts to carry out comprehensive multisectoral economic planning at government level have uniformly failed in that the desired results have not been achieved in the intended manner. The reasons are well known, being basically lack of knowledge to relate programs to one another over time and lack of consent or power to direct the large number of people involved to perform the incredibly large number of actions required to follow the plan. Hence, either the plan is not followed or it does not achieve the intended outcomes.[14] Yet economic planning covers only one of the major components of risk.

Leaving aside government, what do those organizations whose survival depends on correct calculation — capitalist firms — do about risk? Do they attempt comprehensive calculation of the risks in their environment or do they rely on different sources? The evidence against comprehensive calculation is overwhelming. Though everyone would like to maximize profit, no one knows how. Calculating where marginal cost would equal marginal revenue is too expensive and inaccurate to justify the effort.[15]

The operational rule of industrial firms that enables them to act is precisely to avoid attempting to know too much about future consequences. Limiting data, not expanding them, is their guide. Most possible alternatives and consequences are ignored. If there is any finding that has been amply documented in studies of decision making by large-scale organizations of the hierarchical kind, it is that most alternatives most of the time are not considered as candidates for adoption.[16] Only a few ideas—those best known and closest to existing programs—are given attention. The search for knowledge may be widened but only under extreme difficulty. Searching usually stops when something a bit better appears to turn up. Indeed, the first thing to go during economic declines is long-term planning.[17]

In hierarchies goals are multiple and vague, their multiplicity making it easier to satisfy different elements of the firm and to retrospectively rationalize[18] whichever ones happen to be accomplished. Their vagueness facilitates agreement on changing direction without appearing to go back on commitments. By setting modest goals, goals that get the firm by, aspiration levels do not rapidly outrun achievement. If and when the firm approaches them, goals can be raised marginally. It is also unnecessary to meet all goals at once as if the firm were trying to solve a simultaneous equation. There is, as Stafford Beer says,[19] sequential attention to goals, first one, then another. Moves are incremental, working with knowledge of levels achieved in the past to do a little more or less. Decision making is remedial (dealing with difficulty) and serial (as the same problems are attacked over and over again).[20] Unless things are visibly bad, standard operating procedures may be used for most matters. The selection of risks worth taking and avoiding is made by a process, not by a person. Problems are solved in sequence. The need that seems most urgent in these conditions is the one whose solution is realistically feasible. This automatically limits the time frame of decision making and the time frame of perceiving problems. So long as the hierarchy can control the future by planking down its procedures, it makes its expectations for a rational order come true. The result may be very stable over time. So long as no major upheavals are escaping its notice, it will succeed in extending the present into the future. But its information is so heavily filtered that it easily misses a point. To quote another Pearl Harbor example from Allison:

> By December 7, Admiral Kimmel, the Pacific Fleet Commander, had received the following information: a warning from the Navy on November 27, about possible attack, report of a change in Japanese codes (evaluated as very unusual), reports of Japanese ships in Camranh Bay, orders to be alert for Japanese action in the Pacific, messages deciphered from Japan's most secure code ordering Japanese embassies to destroy secret papers, FBI notice that the local Japanese consul was burning papers, government authorization to destroy all American codes and secret papers in outlying islands, and personal warnings from Admiral Stark in Washington. Assuming honesty and competence, a Model I analyst would be led to predict: (1) the fleet would be out of the harbor, (2) the island would be air patrolled, (3) the emergency warning center would be staffed, and (4) the Army would have been notified under the Joint Coastal Frontier Defense Plan. But each of these predictions would have proved incorrect. Instead the Navy's activity on December 7 was identical with its behavior on December 6, which differed imperceptibly from its behavior on December 5, and so on. Each of these details represents standard outputs of an organization functioning according to very established routines.[21]

No such hierarchy can perceive the unexpected. No amount of improved labeling or better spelling out of the instructions will help this kind of perceiver take political information aboard. The fault in perception has nothing to do with the way the message is packaged. It is inherent in the institutional structure.

Individuals in such a society make it work by subscribing to common values. They first value the organization and its long-term future. They value their traditions and rules. They believe that all humans are at least rational enough to follow rational instructions. In a sense the hierarchical way of life is a choice. The people who share the values which uphold it could choose chaos, they could choose to be fired, or they could elect a gang leader to terrorize them. At any moment, a hierarchy could be transformed into something else. If it endures recognizably and reappears irrepressibly at all times in history with the same strengths and weaknesses, this is because it is a feasible way for a large number of people to collaborate. When trying to convince other people about a course of action, they hear themselves pronounce on the long time-span available for decisions—there is no hurry; they hear themselves pronounce on human intelligence—humans are more fallible than institutions; they hear themselves advocate remedies—people need good regulations. They invoke old traditions. The shared fear that is unnecessary to speak is that the hierarchy may collapse. They know what kind of behavior threatens it.

We shall better see what sort of risk portfolio this produces when we can compare it with the alternative, opposed form of organization: the individualistic market. Utility theory was devised to explain the behavior of individuals operating in an entirely individualist society. We can take it that in such a society the individual is an entrepreneur seeking to optimize at the margins of all his transactions. To pursue his best strategies he needs some measure of autonomy. But in such an environment he cannot claim autonomy for himself without setting it up as universally valuable, a right of his fellow citizens, too. He will claim for everyone the rights freely to contract and freely to withdraw from contractual obligations, so long as the procedures for contracting and withdrawing are publicly accepted. For his kind of society, by definition, refuses to give some individuals a hereditary or other right to exact privileges or to turn the free market into monopoly. To keep a free-market environment alive, individual goals should be clear.

Anyone trying to work such a system will recognize that clarity and rankability of goals make negotiations easier and that this will be promoted by any method of standardizing measures of costs and rewards. A monetarized economic system

will help the calculations, though they can be done with pigs or
land or drinks. It helps to be able to separate the transactions,
at least notionally, and to be able to terminate contracts when
they become unprofitable. So the values of equality and individual self-help will be proclaimed by all except the losers.
Everyone would have the same sorts of problems in this society.
They would all know the need to keep up their own visibility.
They would all be seeking credit, offering their support to the
most desirable partners, and screening out uncreditworthy colleagues. Among solutions to their common problems, they
would introduce standard measures and get legislation to protect the measures. They would manipulate the time dimension, pushing repayments into some calculable but distant
future. From these common strategies would emerge some
common values. One shared value would be the exchange system, as such, and then a trust in quantification, as such. Another principle would be to expect the state to see fair play,
protect contracts, protect the standard measures, and ratify
decisive contests. Another high value would be set on personal
success. Inevitably, common values arising out of common
strategies would produce a common pattern of fears. The individualist fears the loss of resources in the market, which would
prevent him from operating independently. He would fear any
threat to the exchange system. These are deep fears, corre-
sponding to hierarchists' fears for the life of his organization.

The behavior that works best in this environment does not
ignore or regret uncertainties; on the contrary, uncertainties
are opportunities. The individualist's attitude toward time is a
response to competitive pressures: he is always short of time.
He has to be ready to cut his losses, so he does not live by history and tradition. His environment does not encourage him to
plan far ahead, nor can he in any way impose his plan on the
future. Other people vary, some quicker, some slower, some
luckier than he. He has to believe in luck. Knowing that he
screens out and drops weak partners and knowing that he himself is subject to screening and dropping, he is not likely to
believe in a uniform human nature. Some are more endowed

than others with cleverness or luck. Apart from this, his ideas of human rationality conform to the classic assumptions of utility theory—to rank objectives, choose the one with the highest value, and go for it.

In spite of all these ways that the individualist's views differ from those of the hierarchist, the two have some similar ideas about danger. Both give priority to any threat to the whole system, whichever it is. Both are sensitive to the public confidence that maintains it. Both like to protect universalistic rules, but the hierarchist wants rules of instruction, while the indivdualist wants fair-play rules that do not stipulate what is to be done. Both have imperialist tendencies, since both can solve their organizational problems by expanding the field of operations—bigger markets, larger collectives. Individualist is more committed to quantification as a method of stating problems; hierarchist will accept the method of quantification once it has become a part of protocol, but he is less impressed with quantification in general since he believes in a limit to calculation. For different reasons, both have a low opinion of the private individual's capacity to reach rational decisions. They disagree on their sense of history: hierarchist will not hurry, traditions have worked well so far; but individualist is in a hurry and has no reason to trust tradition. In a contest, hierarchist may defeat individualist by the sheer power of delay. Though neither is disposed to worry about the distant future, individualist can get attention from hierarchist by making his own case one to which the least complicated protocol applies, as well as by invoking threats to public confidence. With all their differences, hierarchist and individualist agree so well on so many procedures and objectives that the interests of the ordinary man in the street can be overridden when they negotiate directly with each other.

The people want clean air. They want good visibility. They do not want acid rain in their lakes and rivers, nor do they want mountains of waste sludge from purifying processes. In 1970 Congress gave the EPA responsibility to clean the air. The major source of pollutants are coal-burning plants, which

contribute 48 percent of all electric power in the United States
— a share that is likely to grow. The EPA concentrated on the
problem of sulfur dioxide emissions. It could place a ceiling on
the proportion of pollutants emitted by coal burners. This
would leave the producers free to choose the most economical
way of reaching the standard. The dirtier the coal used, the
more expensive the predictable shift to cleaner coal that would
not need additional, expensive purifying machinery. The costs
of transporting cleaner coal would be traded against the costs
of installing purifiers. Two huge political issues arise at once.
First, if a standard of permitted pollutants is to be imposed
nationwide, there is nothing to stop power plants from operating up to these levels in areas that had been completely clean
before. A nationwide standard does not protect air quality that
is already above the standard. Second, the coal of America is
not uniform in its load of sulphur. Eastern coal is much dirtier
than western coal. A ceiling regulation would encourage utilities to buy from the west and pay the extra shipping. The EPA
finds itself threatening the eastern coal interests. To protect
the existing clean air regions, the EPA could drastically lower
the nationwide standard. This brings it up against the utilities,
which see all costs increasing. And it is up against the Energy
Department which opposes a $4 billion annual burden on any
hopes of reaching independence in energy resources. But true
to hierarchical modes of thought, the EPA defined its problem
as if political issues did not exist. It espoused engineering solutions as if adherence to protocol would fulfill its responsibilities. In the end, after much controversy, a relatively high
nationwide ceiling on emissions was adopted, plus a universal
requirement to install scrubbers to protect the clean-air
regions. But at the end of it all, they have been concentrating
on reducing SO_2 when SO_4 may be the major threat.

The culture of hierarchy explains the blinkers and obstina-
cies of the regulatory agency. The culture of individualism
explains the strange yoking of the environmentalists' clean-air
movement with the utilities and the eastern coal interests to
produce a 1979 EPA "decision that will cost the public tens of

billions of dollars to achieve environmental goals that could be reached more cheaply, more quickly and more surely by other means. Indeed, the agency action is so inept that some of the nation's most populous areas will enjoy a *worse* environment than would have resulted if the new policy had never been put into effect."[22] We have to wait till the next chapter to explain why the clean-air movement contributed to this result, which actually runs counter to their intentions and only serves the interests of their opponents, the eastern coal producers and the utility companies.

The difference between the hierarchists' outlook and that of the individualists is to some degree complementary. Though both see the present differently, both like different aspects of it, and both want to see it go on unchanged. Neither is really worried by threats, in the long term. The hierarchist cannot envisage the continuity of past and present being seriously threatened. He expects that the same stable social system that has protected his people so well in the past will be able to do so in the future. It is not that he is willing to let the future go to hell. Just the opposite. By maintaining the advantages of the hierarchy in the present, he is, in his view, giving future generations the best possible protection. The individualist has been watching a scene that he sees changing kaleidoscopically from day to day. He is used to change. The individualist asks nothing better than to take on responsibility for long-term risks, so long as the risk taker is the one allowed to collect the rewards. He does not thank legislators who want to protect him from his folly. On the contrary, legislative interference with market transactions will prevent important new discoveries. With his evolutionary faith that the market will select the best and reject the worst, the individualist feels confident that his activities will leave the future better off. In a sense, he is future oriented; he places his bets on guessing right. But that does not mean explicit concern about the future. Interest rates valuing present versus future returns tell him all he needs to know.

Both individualist and hierarchist can reasonably expect that threatening dangers of the long term may never materialize. The hierarchist expects to be dead by the time any long-run risk materializes, and if still alive, he is not likely to be singled out for blame. His institutional arrangements stop mutual recrimination. Practices of collective decision making encourage secrecy; awkward inquiries are banned and, anyway, the institution is too ponderous to change course lightly. By and large, both risk portfolios can carry a large amount of long-term, low-probability risk. In the traditional view, bureaucracy is extremely cautious and risk averse. Our way of analyzing its perceptual processes suggest the opposite. It is never deliberately risk seeking, but its blind spots make it take risks because it cannot see them. The individualist in the market is traditionally supposed to be risk taking, by full intention and by calculation of profit. Again, and for different reasons, their bias on risks coincides. The hierarchist can take free-lance entrepreneurs and brokers for advisers because there is sufficient understanding between them on the long term: neither is going to be jittery about some threat of remotely probable danger. And each expects its social organization to survive and to do as well by future generations as it has by the past. As to high probability risks, again both would be equally averse to dangers they can see and especially to those that threaten radical change in the fabric of society. Foreign invasion and economic decline are the risks they most fear. Thus they unite on defense but disagree on the extent to which government should impose rules on individual behavior. Whereas the hierarchist chooses not to hear anything that is going on outside and is not disposed to believe it when he does, the individualist is sensitive to rumors. He picks up the news but his short time frame makes his interpretation erratic. The hierarchist who reads his report has a steadying influence. Because they are both concerned to uphold the present social system and neither is able to envisage any different future, they can trust and mutually support each other in regard to environmental risk. Should productivity decline or short-run risks arise from unemployment or inflation, their unity may fall apart.

If we trust our destinies to these kinds of institutions, we know what to expect. The fully individualist society will disregard those who have no past in the league of exchanges. It will manage not to know about the fate of a brother who falls out. Its risk portfolio does not carry heavy fixed liabilities for pensioners, widows, and orphans. It holds people responsible for their own misfortunes; stupidity and neglect explain their losses. Bad luck or guessing wrong about what others want and will pay for is not to be pitied: mistakes bear witness to the costs of leaving behind the worst in order to be left with the best. Individualism strongly believes in the maintenance of the whole exchange system as a prior value: any one individual who threatens it should be penalized. This society is too hasty to be trusted alone with dangerous technology.

To turn in the other direction, we can feel just as unhappy with the hierarchical society. It will also put the maintenance of the whole system above individual survival—this time the system is the bureaucratic organization. It frankly believes in sacrificing the few for the good of the whole. It is smug about its rigid procedures. It is too slow, too blind to new information. It will not believe in new dangers and will often be taken by surprise. It will accept large risks if they appear on a horizon beyond its institutional threshold of concern. These are the typical attitudes of the center, well known in the literature of political science. Values and beliefs emerge as part of the commitment to a form of institutional life. Cultural bias is not floating free but is the part of social exchange that justifies whatever is done. Nothing we have said here about the two center views is new or surprising. Nor is it surprising, given the blindness of the center, that an equivalent analysis has not been established for the border view.

VI

The Border is Alarmed

Social limits to curiosity are drawn so that central institutions can trundle along for many generations without being thrown off balance by alarms and crises. Any rational outlook always includes blinkers. The shortcomings of the vision of individualists and hierarchists have naturally drawn a lot of scholarly attention. What can be said about them is mostly well known. By contrast, the social sources of fundamental criticism (the opposition to individualism and hierarchy) have been curiously neglected. If institutional forms imply strategies and values, analysis that works for the center will also apply to the border.

To identify the risk portfolio of a more dissident view, we have to thread our way through the immense literature on secular and religious protest movements and sects and communes of all kinds. The real borders of society, those places remote from power and influence, do not necessarily have anything to say about society at large. Often people have joined in groups for the purpose of shunning it. When these closed communities speak about the risks ahead, the talk is mostly for each other. Deeply absorbed in their internal politics, they invoke the idea of the evil outside as a theological image, justifying their separation from the established orders.

It is good to realize at once that the concepts of center and border are entirely abstract and relative to the discussion. The sense of border is inherent in the consciousness of the people who perceive their lives as uncommitted and essentially critical of some defined other part of human society where power resides. By contrast, the more a community is closed off from the outside, the more autonomous it is in its management and the more it sits at its own center. A little hierarchy, ignoring the outside, it is too absorbed in its daily affairs to take up the role of border gadfly. Not all small sects behave as border posts, criticizing and warning against the iniquity of the rest of society. On the contrary, many are hierarchies for which the whole outside world only counts as foreign parts for which they are not responsible. The more they are separated from the outside world, the more they tend to adopt the typical procedures and solutions of hierarchy and make its typical assumptions. They do not speak with a distinctive border voice unless their autonomy is encroached upon by a center-focused authority.

The scholars cited in the last chapter assumed that the hierarchical (bureaucratic, organizational) style of thinking and acting is a response to problems of scale. For the sake of easier exposition, we have so far let that pass without comment. But here we suggest that the essential characteristics of hierarchy, purblind and blundering but generally surviving, are to be found also in very small groups where it is less plausible that hierarchical principles have been adopted as a solution to problems of very large scale and complexity. We suggest that hierarchy is a solution to the problems of voluntary organization. A fully voluntary group has organizational problems that make it incapable of sustained responsibility. When some external pressure significantly reduces the voluntariness of membership, typical hierarchical procedures are invented. Bureaucratic compartments can be set up, and the universal rules and standard operating procedures developed; instead of personal leadership, authority is invoked. As soon as (and insofar as) such external pressures appear, a voluntary organization changes its character towards hierarchy. If this is right, then by contrast, the voice from the border is conditioned by the voluntariness of the terms of group membership. We call this third type of rationality *sectarian*. Born of the conditions of voluntary membership and explained by the strategies necessary for surviving in such groups, its perspective on life and on risks contrasts systematically with collectivism and individualism.

To illustrate how a small hierarchical sect can reserve its voice for its own affairs and treat the people of the technologically developed outside world as benighted foreigners, compare the history of two Anabaptist groups, one of which became a little hierarchy, while the other tried to deal with the difficulties of voluntary organization.

In sixteenth century Europe, the Anabaptists originally made their stand on the border of Protestant state organization by rejecting infant baptism. They claimed that anyone entering the Christian communion must be old enough to make a solemn contract on his own behalf. In other words, they strongly preferred voluntariness as a condition of membership. What may seem to us now as a straightforward religious issue was, in fact, a direct political challenge to the Protestant states and their established churches. In those days baptism, not entry on the civil registry of births and deaths, was the civil enrollment of a person into the state. The Anabaptists also refused military service on grounds of a religious prohibition against violence. Since they also refused to take any oath (swearing being forbidden in the Bible), they could not fail to be seen as a subversive element. As a result they endured despoliation, torture, martyrdom, and in 1529, banishment from the Holy Roman Empire. Never left in peace, the Anabaptists were dispersed as refugees in Moravia, Russia, and Switzerland.

The Hutterites were a Moravian group of Anabaptists whose plight was greatly improved in 1553 when, following Jacob Hutter, they formed a community with all their goods in common. They came to the New World about 100 years ago, first settling in South Dakota, where there are still fifteen colonies, and later moving to Canada. The Amish were founded later, in 1693. Their founder, Jacob Amman, divided a much stricter, conservative community away from the other Anabaptists in Switzerland. In the early 1700s, accepting William Penn's offer of land and freedom, the Amish migrated to the New World to live together as brothers according to the New Testament. Though they are the younger foundation, they have been in the United States for much longer, so let us start with their case.

Recall that the Amish were expressly formed to observe godliness more strictly and that brotherliness, that is equality, was always a top value. The first thing to note about the present-day Amish is the ardor with which they still reject social distinctions and put up with inefficiency and hardships for the sake of equality. They avoid creating a priestly class: each man is equally called by God to the same priesthood. They also reject the modern world and all its works completely. Unlike the Hutterites, however, they do not hold their goods in common. Each married man is supposed to have his own farm. Each family is a separate economic unit. They sell to each other at lower prices than to outsiders and lend to each other at lower rates of interest. Investment outside the community is discouraged, with good reason, since surplus earnings are retained to be lent for low interest to young members. They do not use commercial insurance but have well-developed church insurance schemes.

The Old Order Amish prefer 100-acre farms. This is uneconomical in the conditions of the Midwest, where benefits of scale give their competitors a huge advantage. Insofar as their strength lies in intensive farming, this choice confronts these Amish with a natural barrier to expansion. They oppose any of their brethren enlarging his land holdings or buying more than one farm. They consistently forbid rubber tires on buggies or farm equipment because better transport would make it easier to get from one farm to another and so to operate more than one farm. The underlying reason is to protect the principle of equality among brethren. Because they fear the development of a tenant class, they place an upward limit on profits.[1] You might say they perceive this as a risk to their future. Being squeezed out economically first means being squeezed to a lower standard of living. This is not a risk that will unduly worry them. But being unable to split, expand, and buy new land ought to worry them, as we shall see. The real threat to their way of life lies in the need for capital for new investment in land, for settling new communities. Amish settlements have been known to fail. This risk is one which they do not see because institutional blinkers of the sectarian sort make them believe that their constitution could work admirably if only humans were not such backsliders from holiness.

Each district has a so-called bishop, who is responsible for seeking the unanimous opinion of all members. Consistent with their rejection of specialization, the bishop is a farmer like the others, without special qualifications. One Anabaptist historian says that "an unpaid and untrained clergy, too busy with their own affairs to attend to the needs of their flocks" led to a regular loss of members to other churches.[2] Others agree that the senior bishops brought problems by their ultraconservatism. The bishops were nominated by church members and selected by lot. But frequently dissatisfied with the result, many in the community would try to give God a helping hand by manipulating the lottery or, at least behind the scenes, trying to prevent what they felt would be foolish nominations of undesirable candidates. In spite of lottery and other principles for selecting leaders, these communities are well known for their bitter factions. The causes of their disputes were sometimes ritual matters such as footwashing, sometimes signs of worldliness in a fellow member, detected in the width of a hat band, and sometimes unholy hankering after modern technology. "To one bishop it may be worldly to allow men's hat brims to be less than four inches in width, but to another a three inch brim may be acceptable. One bishop may reject the use of propane gas appliances, while another may feel it is acceptable...."[3] Clearly worldliness is an idea capable of being politicized. As a flexible weapon for rebuking or expelling an unruly member, worldliness explicitly invokes the boundary of the group and the group's border stance, distinct from the immorality of mainstream society.

It is the duty of all Amish to report one another's backsliding; public repentence is the only way to avert excommunication. Historians of the Amish tend to wave aside their anguished controversies, referring to the points at issue as minor matters which only became critical because of the clash of willful personalities, questions which could have easily been settled "given a less egotistical leadership and a more patient brotherhood."[4] We shall defend them against their own historians by showing that no matter how patient the people or how wise the leaders, built upon such an institutional basis, the community has no way to proceed except by accusing one another of sinister alliance with the world outside, thus provoking expulsions and splittings. In one exciting period, Anabaptist Mennonites in Indiana saw "four of their principal leaders discredited, demoted, defrocked or rejected in some other way."[5] These turbulent events are the normal scene for a community of equal brothers, and it is politically unrealistic to expect a fully voluntary society to handle its internal affairs otherwise.

Following the various fissions, the different Amish groups make different accommodations to the outside world and its technology. Between 1923 and 1927, a major split separated the Beachy Amish, who use telephones, electricity, and automobiles, all abjured by the Old Order Amish.[6] They may also have larger farms. The Old Order Amish reject modern farm equipment along with education, cinema, modern clothes, and modern medicine. For our comparison, note how they take a particularly negative attitude toward modern technology. It is not that they are fearful of its physical risks but that they are uninterested in the possible benefits. One of the reasons they give for preferring small farms is that there will not be enough land to go around if they work large farms.[7] Here they are right at second remove. There could be enough land to go around, but they will certainly not be able to afford it. Like the pastoral Hima, resisting a change in their social order for the sake of their peace and freedom, they develop a blindspot on the future and on risks that, to the outsider's eye, already disturb their peace and will soon threaten their freedom. They are afraid that resources will dry up, and they are right that resources will get too expensive for them — unless they squarely confront internal problems of organization.

When we turn to the Hutterites, we see that they face a much more secure future. They did not escape persecution even in the New World. For their refusal of military service in World War I, their leaders were imprisoned and maltreated, and some died. Their rejection of secular education has caused constant clashes with the authorities. But their history on this continent is a long story of successful farming, capital accumulation, and demographic expansion. The secret of their success in keeping alive their original ideas seems to lie in their hierarchical principles. In 1880 there were 443 Hutterites in the United States; by 1950 they had increased to 8,542 because of high crude birth rates and low death rates that are a marvel to demographers.[8] The average colony holds 6,000 acres of land, and the farming equipment is up-to-date and the best that money can buy. Their successful organization largely depends on the recognition that they must save to establish each new generation in land, homes, and equipment. They save enough to endow a new branch colony every generation. They set a limit such that no community shall exceed 150 persons.

Hierarchy is strongly established. By contrast with the Amish on their individual farms, the Hutterite community is very strictly regimented. Summoned by bells, they come to a communal dining hall, sit at tables ranged by sex and age, eat quickly with little talk, and go off to their work. The work is organized in common. They elect a manager in charge of each farm operation: a pig boss, machinery boss, chicken boss, kitchen boss. The women are allocated to work teams under their own bosses and take turns in the fields, kitchen, or laundry. Their exploitative and pragmatic attitude to the outside world allows every type of work to be supported with the best possible equipment. With great emphasis on thrift, they reduce their private consumption to a low level uniformity, dress alike, and have similar houses and furnishings.

Their elected pastor takes the chair for meetings of the Council of Elders, who are the managers of each department of farm production. After the pastor, the next in responsibility is the householder, the community accountant. Each community becomes an independent economic unit soon after it has separated from the parent body. Some of the communities are in the millionaire class, while some others are admittedly in economic difficulties. During the Sunday evening meetings, the community affirms its solidarity and discipline; individual misdoings are reported, rebukes administered, punishments awarded, and expelled members reconciled by renewing their baptismal vows. The marriages take place with partners from other Hutterite communities that are within the *leut,* one of the major traditional divisions of colonies, and the women go to join their husbands. Hutterites are never supposed to marry outside their church.

When the time comes to divide in half, the group ought to do something that is very difficult in a hierarchy — make a political choice. They have anticipated the moment by their high level of saving over an average of two decades, and new lands and equipment have been purchased. Somehow they manage to choose a new pastor. But they make less hang upon the choice because they avoid deciding whether he will go with the new team or whether he will be the one to stay behind in the parent group. Lists of two groups have been drawn up and posted. Individuals are allowed to choose which they join — with due regard for a proper demographic spread. On the eve of departure they have agreed who will be with which group, but they do not know who will go and who will stay. Both groups pack all their bags, and both prepare to depart next day. At morning prayers they draw lots, the winners go off with their endowment, the losers stay behind, and both groups start saving again for the next division.[9] Individual decision making has been limited to choosing one's colleagues.

They have not collectivized the big choice of going or staying, but they have successfully avoided choosing.

Hutterite groups would ideally like to settle about thirty miles apart from one another. But non-Hutterite settlers in their vicinity are jealous of their prosperity. In 1942 the Mormons in South Alberta got a state law passed forbidding them to locate closer than forty miles apart because their rapid expansion was thought to be a threat to other farming communities.[10] In one county the Hutterite Brethren constitute the majority of the population, but their custom forbids them from assuming political responsibility. "No country has tolerated the Hutterites for long. . . . They are a people on the move."[11] This demonstrates that they treat the rest of the world as a mere external environment.

The striking difference in daily life between these two religious groups is that the Hutterites enforce a much stricter discipline: no private ownership; regimentation from morning to night; no private profits; no buying, selling, or lending among themselves. Their social system is more centralized and more regulated than that of the other Anabaptist communities. If we ask why the members put up with it, we come to notice their ingenious devices to avoid tension and conflict. The use of the lottery is not the explanation.

The Amish resort to lottery for choosing their officers, and we saw that they have so little confidence in the outcome that they try to manipulate it. But the Hutterites elect their officers. Evidently the choice is not so fraught with tension that they dare not choose openly. They use lottery for decisions connected with splitting. Their rule that the community should split when it reaches 150 persons is a standard operating procedure of the type dear to bureaucracy. The rule guarantees a feasible scale for their kind of organization. It thus limits the problems of factionalism and leadership that beset the Amish, who split when they quarrel and so tend to split rancorously. The rising generation of young Hutterites need not feel frustrated, for they know that leadership positions are going to double in a short while. The Hutterite community manages to obviate many of the internal political problems that trouble egalitarian societies and does so by typical hierarchical strategies. Their community projects a time-span of at least one generation ahead and endows its children materially. Neither of the two Anabaptist churches prizes material welfare above its religious precepts, but the Hutterites see no conflict between prosperity and their traditional way of life. Indeed, successful investment is as necessary as controlled expansion. They are confident that they can handle social conflicts arising from economies of scale. Modern technology does not pose a threat. They do not reject modern medicine, quite the contrary. The Amish, preferring chiropractors and more natural remedies, go for cures in the winter to warm mineral springs in Arkansas, Colorado, or Montana.[12] When Hutterites are sick the brethren send them to the best and most expensive modern clinics.

Hutterites do not see the value they place on material investment as contrary to the basic principles of their association. They intend to make their next generation self-supporting. Willing the end, they will the means and invest so that their goals will be achieved. The Hutterites are not in danger of dying out. The Amish have severe problems. The former have the outlook of a small hierarchy, the latter of a fully voluntary organization. The essential difference between them is that the Hutterites hold property in common. The rule penalizes voluntary withdrawal: individuals can and do withdraw, but at a heavy cost. The outside world has courts which uphold the community's right not to alienate communal property. This external support to the group boundary makes it sufficiently strong for hierarchy to be practicable. Contrast the Amish freedom to hold individual property, whence, we shall argue, all the other differences flow.

In religious sociology, it is agreed that frequent schism and dissolution are the normal lot of sects and communes. Ronald Knox said "Schism breeds," as if the first split entails the next.[13] That small religious groups do not endure is a commonplace of religious history and sociology. But it goes at variance to a favorite assumption of secular sociology that small groups are privileged in matters of solidarity, consensus, and loyalty compared with large groups. Mancur Olson quotes George Homans's *Human Group* as evidence that "the small group has shown much more durability throughout history than the large group.... The appalling fact is that, after flourishing for a span of time, every civilization but one has collapsed ... formal organizations that articulated the whole have fallen to pieces. The one civilization that has not entirely gone to pieces is our Western civilization, and we are desperately anxious about it. [But] at the level of the tribe or group, society has always found itself able to cohere."[14] This is rhetorical overkill. Homans was writing at the heyday of sociological functionalism. He really believed that the small human group which he idealized was a lasting thing. But when large-scale organization collapses and leaves people in small groups, it does not mean that these same small groups have been there all the time. In fact small groups rise and dissolve with greater speed than large ones. If Olson had not been confronted with one of the unquestioned assumptions of the time—that large scale organization is less likely to survive than small—he might not have excluded from his analysis the religious groups which bear it out so well.

A survey of community experiments in nineteenth century America reported that out of hundreds that were started, only three or four lasted more than 100 years; Oneida, the Harmonists, the Beizelites, the Zoarites, and many others declined and dissolved at the old age and death of their founders.[15] A hundred years of life is not very impressive measured against the continuity of monastic orders that have existed since the ninth century. Rosabeth Kanter's excellent study of commitment counts as successful those American communes which have lasted twenty-five years.[16] Noting that this is only a modest criterion of success, we also note that every one of those that passed her test made a contract on admission to hold property in common and gave no compensation for labor.

The threats to survival come from three sources: internal dissension, failure to recruit new members, and failure to stop defectors. Kanter mentions that the last two were especially acute problems for the celibate communities which could not recruit by natural increase or hold their members by ties of kinship. Some were aided by a language barrier: German-speaking peasants feared a hard time if they cut loose in America. But, running quite counter to these findings, the Shakers were both English in origin and celibate, yet they top Kanter's list of long-lived communities. Our first explanation is that they held property in common and our second is that they created their own form of hierarchy. Holding property in common in itself is not enough. There is also the will to make compartments and regulations which obscure most political issues and lighten the burdens of deciding on issues too hot to avoid. Some of the communities which broke up early never managed to turn the personal authority of their founder into institutional forms. Others gave over their life decisions to committees. The fascinating experiment of the Oneida Perfectionists, which only lasted thirty years, cannot have failed because of their eccentric ideas about sex and marriage. The Mormons had equally unorthodox practices, but their kingdom flourished. The trouble for the Perfectionists came not so much from recruiting or maintaining membership but from the indecisions and weaknesses of their twenty-two standing committees.[17] Nevertheless they failed to find a way of making decisions, so they quietly turned a communistic experiment into a joint stock company.

The contract requiring newly admitted members to surrender to the community all private property and all their rights to compensation for work is the foundation for its future success. Of course, members are still free to leave any day they like, but without means of support. When defectors appeal to the American courts for restitution, the latter generally uphold the rights of the community.[18]

In spite of the high costs, members did leave, as is shown by the court records of their attempts to get restitution. Yet a community which has such a strong grip on its membership hardly meets the full definition of a voluntary society.

The more voluntariness is a live issue, so that dissatisfied members can effectively threaten to withdraw, the more the social unit conforms to the sectarian ideal, as announced by Richard Niebuhr. Sect, he says, is a voluntary association. Members are born into churches but must join a sect. Membership is socially obligatory in a church but not in a sect. Churches are inclusive, sects exclusive. "By its very nature the sectarian type of organization is valid only for one generation. The children born to the voluntary members of the first generation begin to make the sect a church long before they have arrived at the years of discretion. For with their coming the sect must take on the character of an educational and disciplinary institution, with the purpose of bringing the new generation into conformity with the ideas and customs which have become traditional. . . ."[19] Sect and church choose different texts from Paul to justify their views. The sect cites 1 Cor. 12: in Christ there is neither Gentile nor Jew, male nor female, bond nor free. The church cites Rom. 13: "Let every soul be subject unto the higher powers."

By following this distinction we hope to avoid the complicated history of definitions of sectarianism.[20] The degree of voluntariness provides a scale on which we can identify degrees of sectarian organization and associated strategies giving rise to sectarian values.

The word *sect* is neutral. From its Latin origin it merely means a following. Sectarian religion has a much more complex connotation. It suggests a schismatic history, exclusiveness, intolerance, narrow adherence to dissident doctrines, and hostility to the outside world. Sectarian groups tend to be small. We have noticed that some religious sects are conspicuously more short lived and prone to fission than others and that the best survivors tend to have adopted hierarchical forms of organization. Either the more vulnerable form of sect organization is subject to an uninstitutionalized paternal authority of the founder and so forced into chaos as he ages, or it is fraternal and egalitarian. The paternalist sects need no further explanation, either for why they work well initially or for why they disappear eventually. The fraternal sects, however, are interesting because they spring up vigorously and succumb to the same problems at all times and places. We will draw on Mancur Olson's *Logic of Collective Action* to explain their ubiquity, their common style, and their problems.[21]

Olson's theory is about the production of public goods, that is, about a collective product that no member of the collectivity can be excluded from using. All persons in the nation, regardless of whether they pay their taxes, enjoy the benefit of government defense. The theory is that, in the absence of coercion and in the absence of special individual incentives, the rational individual will be reluctant to make a sacrifice for the public good because he will get the benefits anyway, if everyone else contributes. His own contribution will not be missed. If all the members make the same observation and if he wants the benefit strongly enough, however, he should be ready to pay all the cost himself. Thus in the absence of coercion there will be unevenness between members contributing to the public good. Those with the biggest interest will contribute as much as they want for themselves, and the others will tend to enjoy the benefit cost free. The larger the group, the more people will share the public good. If all the members in a large group have an equal interest in seeing that the product is provided, each will realize that his own contribution will make negligible difference to the total cost. The main variables in the theory are size of group, composition of group (equal-interest or unequal-interest members), and costs of organization. The larger the group and the greater the costs of organization, the less chance of the public good being provided at all. The more inequality in interest among members, the more chance that the small-interest members will exploit the large-interest members. Multinational voluntary organizations such as the United Nations and NATO always have difficulty in getting members to bear proportionate costs.

The theory deals with small voluntary movements only incidentally. But since so much of it is concerned with the difficulties a group has in the absence of coercion and so much with problems of scale (number of members and levels of costs), it throws light on the perennial problems of sects.

In this chapter we are not concerned with explaining how voluntary movements organized to provide public goods still seem to succeed where Olson's theory would predict their failure. As we shall see later, the cost of organizing may turn out to be exceedingly low or be unexpectedly subsidized; sometimes selective incentives are provided; sometimes the mass media help to build up the equivalent of small-group, face-to-face social pressures. Our argument here is that Olson seems to have correctly described the dilemmas of voluntary groups, insofar as his theory accounts for their smallness in size and their frequent fission. He expressly excludes religious groups, but we take the liberty of applying the theory across the board to any voluntary groups, religious or secular.

The community contract for signing over all property to the group is a form of negative sanction, voluntarily accepted, equivalent to American workers' wishes to be coerced into supporting a union. Olson contrasts the extremely low participation in labor unions and the overwhelming support that workers give to measures that will force them to support a union. They want the benefits of a strong union, they mistrust their own readiness to pay up, and even when they have bound themselves obligatorily to pay union dues, they still give very little of their own time to union meetings, so the running of it is left to the big-interest members who get some personal satisfaction and prestige from the work. The founder of a commune usually behaves as a big-interest member, carrying most of the burdens of organization.

Apart from size of group, costs of organization, and inequality of members' interests in the production of public goods, Olson goes on to consider a characteristic of the goods themselves. Some public goods are diminished in value as more people have access to them, while the value of others is unaffected.

The first is the case in which the firms are rivals in a restricted market. If one firm gets a larger share of the market, the others must get less. When they agree to raise prices, the fewer firms there are, the greater the benefit to each. This he calls an exclusive group, one which does not welcome new members. By contrast, an inclusive group is organized around a collective product whose value only increases as the group grows. Olson associates the first type, the exclusive group, with market organization and the second with nonmarket organization, such as lobbying. Significantly, we can also add highways and parks to the list of public goods whose benefits are reduced when more people use them. The difference turns upon whether the supply of the collective good increases or decreases when the group expands. For insight into why some religious groups become closed egalitarian communities liable to fission and why they tend to be small in scale and even to peter out, we can consider this distinction between the kind of public goods they are intended to produce for their members. According to how small a role prestige plays in the list of their public goods, some will be mainly inclusive groups, like lobbies, that want to welcome as many as can be persuaded to join, and others will be exclusive groups with the worst problems of voluntary organization. It is to everyone's interest that their number will be as small as possible, yet it is essential that all members participate 100 percent—since any one nonparticipant can take the benefits produced by the collective action of the others. This has the same effect as a constitutional requirement for unanimity in a voting system. Any one member can withhold his little share of input and bargain to get a larger share of the gain. The 100 percent participation, the veto power, the extended bargaining, make group-oriented action even more difficult.

If a sect falls into this dilemma, its members are rivals, yet they depend upon one another for raising the standards of spirituality. Any one of them who does not support their agreed standard of unworldly behavior and strikes out for his own definition of holiness can defeat their efforts. They need 100 percent participation. They impose equality. Their high reputation for a collective product, holiness, that they all can enjoy, attracts recruits—and so on. If these were counted as exclusive groups, according to Olson members would have an ambivalent attitude toward a new entrant. "If the top '400' were to become the top 4,000, the benefits to the entrants would be offset by the losses of old members, who would have traded an exalted social connection for one that might be only respectable."[22] Some of the public goods produced in sects are of the inclusive kind: the more who attend the rituals, who sing and pray and demonstrate that they have been made happier or healed, the better for everyone. Others are of the exclusive kind. Veida Skultans illustrates this with her study of a spiritualist circle. On the one hand, all the members felt they benefited from the spiritual progress of one member; on the other hand, they were all tempted to acquire personal power. The fierceness of the competition for power related to the level of commitment to spiritualism. Anyone whose rewards came solely from that context would be more involved in the power struggle.

One of the attractions of spiritualism is that it deceptively promises high ritual status to all adherents: spiritualist doctrine recognizes the universality of mediumistic or spiritual power in a latent, if not manifest form. Moreover, mediumistic power is the currency in terms of which status within the movement is acquired. However, high status is by definition scarce: if it is too easily acquired, it loses value and thus destroys itself . . . whilst the theoretical universality of mediumistic power is readily acknowledged, its actual manifestations constitute a threat to all committed spiritualists. This threat is increased by the absence of clearly formulated beliefs and structure within the groups. . . . Competition for status exists not only between individual group members, but also between circles and between churches and circles. . . .[23]

Absence of structure signifies the "hung" meetings with holdouts among the 100 percent participating members, the pressure for fraternal equality, the indecision, and the failure to achieve a collective good. Here we have the rationale underlying the behavior of the fraternal sect where membership is entirely voluntary. We also have the explanation of its schismatic tendencies.

Malcolm Calley gives a vivid account of how fission follows disputes about leadership in West Indian Pentecostal sects in England.[24] Continuity and the solidarity of Christian fellowship are valued, whereas causing "dissension among the saints" is condemned as ungodly. When a split occurs, those of both factions claim to represent the original church. A leader seldom admits to having led a breakaway movement; his claim is that he was seceded from. He expresses his authority very indirectly, seeking more to express the mind of the community and to interpret God's laws.

Generally a leader is loth to disfellowship an insubordinate "saint," as by doing so he is losing a member and giving him to some other congregation. But on the other hand he may feel it is better to lose a member than risk having him lead others out of the church. Disfellowship for insubordination alone is rather unusual; it is more usual for the leader to bring other charges as well, very often those of breaking sexual taboos. The split from the Church of the Living God in Reading to form the Pentecostal Church of the First Born came about in just this way. A member challenged the authority of the leader, who retaliated by accusing him of having divorced one wife and married another, which of course is not permissible in these sects. Both contestants then talked with tongues at the same time, one against the other, each trying to demonstrate to the congregation that he was the more holy, that God was on his side. The service . . . ended without either giving ground, despite efforts by other members to act as "peace makers" and heal the breach. The following week I heard that the member had been disfellowshipped, and a month later that he was running an independent organization.[25]

Calley says useful things about the relation of doctrine to the politics of fission. Since a leader, once accepted, is difficult to challenge, a member aspiring to replace him must be willing to split the congregation; and he can contemplate this only if he can find Biblical authority. "The saint tries to discover in biblical terms why he feels restless and dissatisfied. His discovery that the congregation is not 'right with God' reinforces his perhaps unconscious desire to become a leader himself. The doctrinal issue most apt to this purpose that is most often used is 'church government'; it is claimed the congregation is not being run on strictly biblical lines, that authority is more or less centralized than scripture lays down, or that officers and responsibilities are wrongly distributed."[26]

The process of splitting has obvious benefits. It reduces the scale of the unit, it lowers the costs of organization, and it also renews fervor. "Without the constant turmoil of sect formation, building and fission, members would lose interest and the groups would wither and die."[27]

Now we know the special problems of voluntary organization. The difficulty of getting decisions, the bargaining, the readiness to hold out and even to splinter off — all make effective sustained action difficult. This is why the voluntary type of organization is characteristic of the border. It would never be responsible or stable enough to maintain a center. An initial state of voluntariness entails the characteristic pattern of values that emerges to justify this behavior.

The pressure for a 100 percent participation and the insistence on equality, however much loved for their own sake, are demands for equal shares. Thus leadership has to be concealed, or at least the leader has to claim authority from a source that is over human institutions. Stratification, regimentation, and rules are abhorred, unless they are justified by appeal to the higher authority; the unanimous consent of members is not likely to underwrite inequalities. Meeting the minimum costs of organization from the members is an almost insuperable problem. Hence to their initial commitment to equality and individuality is added the value of smallness of scale. The difficulty of making any collective enterprise prosper under these conditions tempts those who are trying to keep the sect together to condemn prosperity: rather the equality of individuals and their free community than material goods that could be had at the price of destroying the character of the community. To heighten the value of its collective

spiritual good, there is the strategy of disvaluing the world outside. Everything turns the sect in upon itself: the sect will endure longer, the more it can control intercourse between its
members and the outside. From this comes a further strategy
for sectarian survival, adding to disdain of the world: fear of
pollution, of cancerous contamination from external intercourse. The threat of danger from outside is used in internal
politics to justify factions and to force expulsions and splits. If
it follows these strategies, the sect will keep itself small and so
keep down the costs of organization.

It is not smallness that is first loved nor a passion for equality
that brings the fraternal sect to pursue its characteristic ends
but the reverse. A losing battle against the difficulties of voluntary organization presses its members into rejecting increase of
scale, preferring egalitarian rulings, and attempting closure
against the rest of the world (insofar as that is possible without
negative sanctions).

This is the organization that speaks out against the injustices
of the center. Attack on the center is a regular phase of its
internal politics. The sectarian can safely criticize behavior
which would be incompatible with sectarian organization.
Since its decision-making processes are unable to sustain a
positive policy, the sect is free to attack any policy so long as it
stays in the attacking posture. It rejects worldly behavior,
counting as worldly the things it cannot afford and seeming to
have voluntarily embraced poverty, whereas poverty followed
from having embraced voluntarism. The conditions of voluntary organization cause sectarians to invoke God and claim
higher spiritual worth than the rest of the world. But it is not
so much that they chose first to criticize the central institutions
and therefore formed the sect. Rather it was the other way
around: they combined voluntarily and, as a result of problems and strategies, they found the scope to criticize. Their
voluntary association puts them in opposition to the individualists and the hierarchists. Inevitably they must see the risks
in the world from a different perspective.

The first difference between the border and center views is

about what the future will be like. The center takes it to be an extension of the present. Sectarians expect discontinuity. They expect a different future and they expect it will be bad. Established society is incorrigibly evil, being both coercive and hierarchical. It must not be imitated and it cannot continue. They have a vested interest in bad news that shows the society outside is polluted and also shows that the sect inside is pure. In the long run the millennium will arrive, but in between then and now there will be floods, quakes, and fires. Sectarians need the future to be different and worse to turn their criticism into warnings and so make them politically more weighty.

Whereas it suits the center to ignore long-term risks and low-probability ones, however big the expected damage, the sectarian is much more alert to them. He assesses the long term as something fairly close and worries about the damage, however low the probability. The threat in the future is part of the sectarian's present political armory against his rivals. He wins adherents if he can threaten bigger dangers and associate them more convincingly to the corruption of the outside world. His political experience of stalemate and veto doubles his dislike of large-scale politics. He has seen followers melt away, lured by a seductive preacher whom he has heard accused of worldly ambition. He himself may have followed or even lured on his own behalf. He knows what the seduction is. All the rhetoric is at hand for denouncing large organization as such.

Now we can set up three distinctive risk portfolios, two typical of the political center, one typical of the border, all bounded by the rational strategies entailed by the organizational principle. The center sees the future as continuous with the present. It has numberless ways of discounting information to the contrary. It expects disturbances and setbacks in the normal course, but it also expects to weather them. In the long run it is optimistic. The border foretells imminent disaster. It does not believe in the long run, and in the short run it is pessimistic. Paradoxically perhaps, it is optimistic about the perfectibility of human nature. Since the border is committed against institutions, it must fall back on faith in human goodness as the basis for good society. When its prophets inveigh against human wickedness, they are calling upon the people to return to their essentially human power of moral regeneration. The center does not worry about possible irreversible damage to nature emanating from its own technology but rather about the possible irreversible destruction of its social systems.

The border is self-defined by its opposition to encompassing larger social systems. It is composed of small units and it sees no disaster in reduction of the scale of organization. It warns the center that its cherished social systems will wither because the center does not listen to warnings of cataclysm. The border is worried about God or nature, two arbiters external to the large-scale social systems of the center. Either God will punish or nature will punish; the jeremiad is the same and the sins are the same: worldy ambition, lust after material things, large organization.

Remember that science is supposed to have replaced God as the source of explanations and threats. Nature as grand comptroller is the next best thing to God. No other cause is so powerful for the sectarian's purpose. Recall that a main concern for everyone in an exclusive, egalitarian, voluntary group is not to get expelled. Another main problem is how to keep the leader from arrogating to himself and his friends benefits produced by the efforts of other members. He has to be blackmailed by factional threats to withdraw. Each member at some time or other may need to defame and join in expelling another. We have recounted how the processes for fission and expulsion work.

For this kind of organization to persist, each sectarian needs the others' concurrence in an image of threatening evil on a cosmic scale: for this, the idea of global, irreversible damage serves well. They also need a model of the godly or good society, the sect itself, to counterpoise against ungodliness or worldliness outside and to justify their control of their own group. They need the idea of conspiracy to accuse disloyal members of plotting with outsiders; the large-scale evilness of the conspiracy is necessary to justify expulsion. Sectarian views on human nature have to be carefully balanced between shock at the discovery of badness and faith in human goodness and power for renewal. The sect needs enemies. It encourages thinking in either/or terms because of the political focus on that dividing line between saints and sinners. Compromise is ruled out because there is only one important distinction, between those who are loyal and the betrayers. Purity becomes a dominant motif. Where other preachers might choose themes of charitable forgiveness, sectarian sermons harp on defilement and purging.[28] If evil does enter the sect, which is good, the evil must have entered secretly, just as the hidden dangers of technology enter and spoil the hierarchy.

The more the community is struggling with the problems of voluntary organization, the more it is inactive, able only to gather force for a series of discrete demonstrations of solidarity against the outside. Spending its energies on disputing, splitting, and preaching to each other, the sect wisely makes a virtue of its poverty. It abjures wealth, which its form of organization prevents it from earning anyway. In a modern society the cultural difference between a sect and a hierarchy shows in their attitudes toward technology. More than anything else, technology represents social distinction, the division of labor, the making of wealth and everything that is prized by the center. We understand the preference of the Old Order Amish for nature cures and their condemnation of rubber tires and similar technological advances. Their organization is sectarian, while the Hutterites are a confederation of little hierarchies.

When we return in the next chapters to assessing sectarian tendencies in contemporary American cultures, we shall find that the same social distinctions accord with the same sets of cultural bias. Some groups in the antinuclear and environmental movement are organized on hierarchical principles. In this case, their values and theories about society and the world, human nature, and technology are more fitted to the culture of hierarchies. Those which are organized as completely voluntary organizations, however, speak more like sects. The more hierarchically organized tend to defend the bits of nature they want for their own use. The sectarian style is to use the whole of nature to solve its problems of voluntary organization; sects attack the center or separate from its contaminating influences.

Given the sectarians' problems, we understand why they identify the risks the world faces from the pollution of nature. Global issues, not local ones, will serve their purpose best. The cause of the handicapped or of unemployed blacks is not so formidable, damage not so irreversible or so vast in scale as to warrant invoking general doom. Sects need to speak on behalf of the whole of mankind, not for a few millions. Physical nature is their best substitute for God, not only because nature is powerful and unpredictable. The bias against elaborate institutional forms makes nature the appropriate good counterpart to defend against bad central society. In this light, Emerson's praise of nature sounds sinister. "Nature is loved . . . as the City of God," he said, adding that nature is loved "although, or rather because there is no citizen."[29] The sacred places of the world are crowded with pilgrims and worshippers. Mecca is crowded, Rome is crowded, Jerusalem is crowded. In most religions, people occupy the foreground of the thinking. The Sierra Nevadas are vacant places, loved explicitly because they are vacant. So the environment has come to take first place.

VII

The Border Fears For Nature

The many groups that exist to mobilize public concern for the evils of our times are organized in various ways. We can demonstrate the social theory of risk perception by classifying them according to their principles of organization. We expect that those which show up as most hierarchical in their relation with each other and the outside world will also be making the more typically hierarchical selection of dangers. Those organized on voluntaristic, egalitarian principles will make the sectarian selection of risks and justify their view of danger with a recognizably sectarian worldview.

Little hierarchies speak and act like big hierarchies. Though they may be intended to protect nature from depredation, theirs is not a true border voice. The more that a public interest group is organized as a hierarchy, the more it believes there is time for reform. It seeks incremental changes and speaks frankly for its own perceived interests. The more like a hierarchy, the stronger its internal control and the less its fear of subversion. The more hierarchical the organization, the less it bears a message about catastrophe and the less it is cosmic in its portent.

A hierarchy can be maintained so long as there are enough selective incentives for individual members so that they have an interest in subscribing without being too concerned with relative status or with who is making the decisions, or how. Or it can be maintained so long as exit from the group is heavily penalized. As we have seen, without these supports it faces the problems of other voluntary groups. It will either suffer the exploitation of the few by the many, or it will have to lower the costs of organization to a point where the members' individual contributions are really negligible and then it will face other problems. One of the ways of collecting more voluntary support for less cost of organization is by invoking danger. Either the backlash of God or the backlash of nature is an effective instrument for justifying membership. If none of these strategies is enough, the group as a last resort can organize itself upon the production of prestige for all members. In this latter case the strategies for survival in an exclusive group exert a powerful pressure towards godliness and utopian, millenarian values.

The sectarian cosmology expects life in the future to undergo a radical change for the worse. It is not confident that the disaster can be averted. There may be no time left. But it knows how the disaster has been caused: corrupt worldliness; that is, ambition for big organization has endangered mankind and new technology represents all that is most reprehensible — social distinctions, the division of labor, materialist values, unfeelingness for individual suffering. Its cosmology is characterized by dichotomized values: good and bad are severely contrasted, compromise is bad, purity is good. Paradoxically, given the alert detection of betrayers in their ranks, the sectarians supplement their mistrust in human organization with trust in the goodness of human individuals. The sect espouses the widest causes, all mankind rather than a section. They refer to God or nature as arbiters to justify their rightness, and every tragedy that can be attributed to worldliness as here defined is chalked up as one more divine or natural warning. We have seen how in a secular civilization nature plays the role of grand arbiter of human designs more plausibly than God. Consequently the environmental movement is the case which should give the best illustration of our theme. Here we find that big differences of organization correspond to big differences in their stated expectations and values.

The conservation movement dates as far back as 1872 when Yellowstone became the first national park. The Sierra Club was founded some twenty years later. By 1908, when the Sierra Club led the fight to preserve the Hetch Hetchy Valley from being converted to a reservoir serving San Francisco, there were seven national conservation organizations in existence, and by the 1920s many new national parks had been established. The efforts of dedicated hunters and fishermen (including President Theodore Roosevelt) caused a series of important laws to be enacted to protect wildlife and create government agencies to manage natural resources. At that stage the conservation movement depended heavily on its big-interest members, and once they had procured enough conservation measures to suit their needs, it seemed to lose momentum. Some organizations were dissolved, while other remained stable with relatively small memberships. A resurgence of interest in conservationism began in the late 1950s and early 1960s when existing conservationist organizations formed coalitions to fight well-publicized battles against developers over the projected Echo Dam at Dinosaur National Monument in 1956 and to protect the California Redwoods, the Cascades in Washington, and the Grand Canyon.

The conservation groups then began to widen their interests to embrace air, sea, and river pollution. Rachel Carson's *Silent Spring,* a book on the environmental damage of DDT published in 1962, strongly roused public interest in conservation. The first national celebration of Earth Day in 1970 mobilized many thousands of Americans who attended rallies and took part in numerous local environmental activities. Ecology having entered American consciousness, a number of new national and local organizations sprang up. Today there are some seventy-five national environmental groups and thousands more at state and local levels.

Environmental issues are ideal for a loose federation of small voluntary groups. They are sufficiently numerous, diverse, and complex to allow each group to specialize. For example, in 1977 the Sierra Club led the campaign on water pollution legislation, the Environmental Defense Fund campaigned to prevent the slaughtering of porpoises by tuna fishermen, while Environmental Action demanded legislation against no-deposit bottles. Each major national organization implicitly recognizes this informal division of labor by joining coalitions led by the principal campaigner on each issue. Such cooperation is helped by the fact that in recent years all of the national groups have built up large lobbying staffs in Washington whose members are personally acquainted with their counterparts in other groups.

One important difference between the modern environmental movement and its conservationist predecessors is the professional staff that now supplements the voluntary efforts of members. Before 1950 some, such as the National Audubon Society and the National Wildlife Federation, employed full-time, paid staff members. They were very few, principally involved in administration, and none were full-time lobbyists. In the past ten years the Sierra Club has moved further toward hierarchy by developing a national complement of eighty-five full-time staff members including support personnel. The growth in staff coincided with a dramatic increase in membership. The period of major growth occurred between 1965 and 1971, coincident with the upsurge in public environmental awareness. The rate has been considerably slower since 1972, with most of the national groups maintaining their membership at about the same level or continuing to grow at a more modest rate.

Direct-mail appeals are the primary means of recruitment used by the national groups. Although for many years it relied primarily on recruitment through its local chapter organization, the Sierra Club, for example, has taken to campaigning for its members in this way. The various national organizations send out annual appeals to people who are likely to be sympathetic to the cause. They are offered the chance to support the different groups' lobbying, educational, and legal efforts. They may also enjoy some private benefits, which usually include a publication and sometimes the opportunity to purchase merchandise at a discount or to go to organized outings. According to Robert Mitchell's researches, only a small proportion of members takes advantage of these private benefits.[1] At the national level the members play a relatively passive role. Their numerous small contributions combine to represent a substantial part of the national organizations' financial support. Members form a constituency which the groups can claim to represent in their lobbying; and some of them can be mobilized periodically to write letters, send telegrams, or make phone calls to legislators in support of key bills.

The members themselves seem to be mainly white, middle-class, professional people. While there may be some variation in the dominant age group from one organization to another, the popular stereotype of the youthful environmentalist does not seem to be borne out by systematic research. The political party affiliation of environmentalists is distributed in much the same way as among the general population.[2] Within this general framework there is significant diversity in the organizational styles. The older conservationist organizations, such as the Sierra Club and the National Audubon Society, tend toward hierarchy. On the other hand, as we shall show, the newer and more aggressive environmental groups are modeled more suitably for speaking for the border in a typically sectarian frame of ideas.

When David Brower became full-time director of the Sierra Club in 1952, it had about 7,000 members. By May 1969 the Club had grown to about 77,000. He had led several large-scale campaigns, including those to save the California Redwoods and to prevent two reservoirs from being built on the Colorado River near the Grand Canyon National Park. The public lobbying for the Grand Canyon campaign had led the Internal Revenue Service to withdraw from the Sierra Club its tax-exempt, charitable status. Resentment against Brower's militant style of leadership and against some of his accounting practices brought about a serious split in the leadership. The 1969 board election was a battle fought for two clearly defined slates: the Concerned Members for Conservation (CMC) and the Active Bold Constructive (ABC) slate. William Devall, who studied the dispute, stated: "The election was seen as a competition between factions of the elite in the club rather than a true grass-roots opposition to a long-established and monolithic incumbent administration."[3] The CMC stood on the platform of strict financial control, a volunteer board as distinct from paid staff, and a gentlemanly approach to campaigning that included inviting the opposition to dinner. The ABC slate demanded the end of "the California elite's rule," the end of the hiking-club image, and a move toward an aggressive concern with total environment and global conservation issues.

> Though the old-time conservationists may understand that there is a crisis . . . they still want to be gentlemen while the world is dissolving. We know what doesn't work: the quiet, gentle approach. . . . The world is going to tumble around its ears if the Sierra Club — or someone — doesn't do a job in the next five years. If the Sierra Club's main worry is the preservation of its own existence, there won't be any environment left for it to exist in.[4]

> The old liners are all right on most issues . . . but not those that come in conflict with their personal lives, their friends, the people they see at cocktail parties. They argue, "we must have pleasant and fruitful discussions with the people trying to wreck the landscape so they won't do it so bad." We should appeal not to the lobbyist but to the public at large — on TV, in the press. Gentle persuasion does not work. The utilities have to be controlled, not reasoned with.[5]

Note that while the world is tumbling and dissolving, there is no time for gentleness or reasoning. Here we see how the form of the organization determines what is reckoned a disaster. The Sierra Club consistently expressed the typical concerns of hierarchy, according to which the worst eventuality is to change the structure of the society.

The election result favored the more conservative platform

by a majority of two to one. One board member felt that un-controlled growth would destroy the structure of the Sierra Club and that no benefits to the environment were worth that. "We believe what Brower is doing, whether it makes money or not, is heading the Club towards disaster. Brower's ideas have no place for the amateur, and the Sierra Club is unique be-cause it is an amateur, a volunteer organization."[6]

Although he remained as a member of the Club, Brower was forced to resign from the Board. At this point many doubted whether his charismatic style of leadership could continue without the Club name, power, and resources behind him. But the skeptics were proved wrong. Within sixty-nine days Friends of the Earth was founded with a fifteen-member board of directors and an executive committee of six board members authorized to establish policies. By creating a group around a self-perpetuating elite, Brower had avoided having his hands tied by the kind of bureaucracy which he believed held back the development of the Sierra Club. Devall described Brower's organization principles as an explicit rejection of hierarchical principles.

Don't be tied up with bureaucracy and what sociologists call "organi-zational maintenance," because the organization becomes an end in itself. Brower liked to select good people and give them their freedom to do their job. The Sierra Club, on the other hand, in its structure and processes, has grown as complex, bureaucratic and heavy with job descriptions, committees, chains of command and administra-tion as the government organizations and private corporations with which it battles.[7]

Friends of the Earth (FOE) has led major campaigns against nuclear power, pollution, exploitation of Alaska, and a host of other causes to protect the environment. From its inception, FOE emphasized its long-range concern by developing interna-tional affiliation. A primary disagreement between Brower and the Sierra Club had been over the international role Brower wanted the Club to adopt. While emphasizing the importance of its global cause, FOE leaders have also insisted that it remain decentralized. Its international organization remains a network of autonomous and varied sister groups sharing a common name and purpose.

The determination to remain decentralized has also affected the character of its local chapter organization. FOE rejects tax-deductible status and does not seek support from wealthy individuals or foundations. Its local branch organizations supply most of its funds. They are relatively autonomous and, conversely, they have very little control over the national organization. The FOE inner leadership maintains its position of power and a broad membership (over 24,000) partly by emphasis on the autonomy of local branches and partly through its procedures for elections. These are held at the annual general meeting, which all individual members are entitled to attend. Financial aid is not provided for those who have to travel great distances, nor are branches empowered to send representatives; but FOE makes extensive use of the proxy vote system by which individuals return a form to FOE headquarters empowering the leadership to act on their behalf. Within FOE there has been some disquiet about this procedure, but as yet the directors have not chosen to use the provision in the constitution to allow ballot by mail.

Although FOE is formally democratic, there seems to be little opportunity for members to participate actively in national decision making. At the local level it is loose and decentralized, but at the national level the leadership continues as a small, active elite. Rather than promoting the organizational growth and stability valued so highly by the Sierra Club, this leadership favors reliance on a dedicated and generous staff and on volunteers, which enables FOE to concentrate its financial resources on achieving particular goals.

Here we can note several sectarian tendencies: a favoring of equality against leadership, fear of infiltration, jealousy, and fear of ambition. Finally we recognize the old utopian hopes of peace through moral regeneration.

FOE local chapters maintain a high level of participatory democracy. The group rejects a traditional committee structure for its local organization. Rather than electing representative committees to carry organizational responsibilities, FOE local chapters prefer a division of labor based on a number of task forces, each specializing in a particular function such as fund raising or recruitment. Task forces are self-selecting, each chapter member being free to decide which sort of activity suits him best.

The hostility and bitterness which marked the split in the Sierra Club have rarely been displayed in its subsequent relations with FOE. Both have participated jointly in coalitions on major issues. Brower has continued his Club membership and, for its part, the Club has valued Brower's contribution to the environmental cause. They even presented him with the John Muir award in 1977.

Environmental groups generally agree that coalitions, both among themselves and with groups having diverse but not opposing views, are valuable and necessary to achieve their goals. Although it will ally with other conservation organizations for particular objectives, FOE will never merge or compromise its separate identity for the sake of a unified movement.

If we grant for the sake of argument that a unified movement would be ideal, is there any reason to suppose that conservationists could achieve this ideal? The peace movement is not unified, nor are the denominations that call themselves "Christian." If unity could be achieved, it would surely be temporary. A unified conservation movement would immediately begin fragmenting again, not only because of human cussedness, but also because of the perfectly sincere and plausible belief by separatists that the super-organization was handling one issue after another less effectively than would more sharply focused individual organizations. If plurality didn't exist, we'd have to invent it. [8]

They believe that a multiplicity of organizations is more likely to ensure that important local issues receive their due attention, which they would never get from a national organization. Furthermore, the existence of specialized organizations with expertise in particular issues is seen as strengthening the overall movement. Finally, environmental groups are afraid of infiltration and subversion by corporate interests.

Adversaries could concentrate all their fire on a single super-organization, and when they defeated it on an issue like the SST, for instance, they'd dispose of all conservationist opposition at a single stroke. A super-organization would also be vulnerable to subversion — and don't for a moment think that well-heeled adversaries are too pure to bore from within! There is safety in numbers. A conservation movement consisting of many organizations is a much more difficult target to catch in a cross-fire, and because less can be gained by it, there is less temptation for opponents to bore from within. Subversion of an individual organization would leave today's conservation movement substantially intact, whereas subversion of a super-organization would leave the movement in a shambles.[9]

FOE claims that government, industry, and the public at large must be made aware of the immediate and severe danger to the environment, or else the earth will not survive for anyone.

FOE is not an end in itself. It exists to reduce the impact of human activity on the environment and to ensure that we as a species adopt policies which permit life in its varied and beautiful forms to continue. But FOE cannot thrive in isolation any more than a single species can; we are, and need to be, part of a political ecology. We must thoroughly understand the basic limits of the political world in which we live. We must know our relationship to the other components of that system, benign and hostile, and we must learn to act appropriately to our surroundings. We cannot force the world to adopt our views, values and policies, but we can construct, together with other institutions, a web of political life that will have no place for exploitative values, destructive technologies, and dehumanized relationships.[10]

This definition of its aims leads Friends of the Earth to stress that allies should be sought outside of the field of conservation. Consumers, public-interest groups, labor unions, religious organizations, and minority associations are pursued with the aim of obtaining support. It seems logical that the broader the scope of groups supporting a cause, the more seriously will established politicians have to consider it. Thus FOE has shown greater conscious interest in recruiting the support of blacks and labor than more established conservationists.

The first thing to do is to get the endorsements of national environmental, consumer, and public interest groups. Such endorsements will give you credibility. . . . Don't stop with environmental or consumer groups: labor unions, religious organizations, and fraternal organizations often can be persuaded to take stands on national issues. These groups sometimes have more impact than public interest groups. The broader the scope of groups supporting your cause, the more seriously the Congressman will consider it. When you have a broad coalition of support, it is difficult for him to say "those do-gooders are at it again."[11]

Despite its elitist national structure and its largely pragmatic motive for enlisting support from groups outside the conservation movement, FOE maintains an almost utopian vision of future society in which all forms of life will exist harmoniously without political, economic, and technological restraints. We hear the sectarian overtones of love, cosmic unity, and resistance to center machinations:

In each new country we would try to find people with the right bias toward the planet and the things that live on it, people who also had a gift of leadership to match their devotion, people who knew what would work in their respective countries. The principal coordination would be spiritual, with one goal — the preservation, restoration, and rational use of the earth.[12]

We note the determination to remain small and decentralized. We note the sectarian tendency to concentrate all kinds of disparate issues into one inclusive doctrine.

If one has to boil it down to one issue, I guess that issue is Growth. Growth of population, of technology, of economy, of waste, of products, of per capita consumption, of power, of things generally.

They're all so interrelated. Wisdom, spirit, freedom, well-being—
these are the things that need to grow. Let's face it, bigger and better
are probably antipathetic at this point in human history.[13]

The world view of FOE is of a carefully balanced ecosystem
that is being blindly upset by man with potentially disastrous
social and physical consequences. Although FOE rejects the
idea that its own organization may serve as a model for future
society, its long-term vision is a harmonious world modeled on
its concept of balanced interrelations in nature.

By contrast, the Sierra Club has always been prepared to
make compromises with economic demands in its campaigning. Its membership sees conservation as only one among a
number of legitimate concerns. The single, inclusive aim of
FOE to bring man back into balance with the environment on
a worldwide scale concentrates all the issues together.

FOE ideas of political activity are strictly border ideas, from
people who mean to operate permanently on the border—
lobbying, litigation, and nonviolent obstruction. Its coalitions
are temporary and action oriented, never mergers. It will not
pick its adversary or set out a list of administrative goals. Making a program is center strategy; attacking center programs on
behalf of nature, God, or the world is border strategy.

FOE is an extremely successful movement. We have to wait
to see how it will measure on the scale of longevity—thirty
years will be enough for their purposes, since they expect the
future to collapse very suddenly if they are not successful. We
predict that they will fail if their overriding goal is to preserve
the sectarian character of their movement, as such. When that
happens, a movement loses effective power by diffusing
authority. It also loses direction by attacking its leaders. It
loses contact with the world it wants to change by setting up
barriers against it.

The antinuclear movement presents an even clearer example of the sectarian cosmology emerging from a voluntaristic,
egalitarian association. Alain Touraine, after studying the
French antinuclear movement and its connection with the

ecology movement, reproaches them for never producing any program for society, never identifying adversaries or moving to engage constructively with urgent problems.[14] They make a stand against abuses and against particular projects, but on the positive side they do not go beyond abstractions, justice, freedom from repression, humanity—who would not support such a list? We have seen that when sects give their own organizational problems the highest priority, these attitudes are solutions. They must avoid a program; if they had one, they might be called upon to implement it. If they name their adversary, they might defeat him, in which case they would be faced with conflicting moral principles. If they were to engage with the central institutions of society, they would have to stop vilifying the social process as such. They would have to stop accusing their own members of treasonable conspiracy. Without their usual tactics for mutual control, their sectarian organization would be in jeopardy. They might even need someone to lead from the front, in which case they would have to break the habit of dragging down anyone who seems to be taking more of that scarce commodity, the prestige of the movement. Solutions to the problems of voluntary organization entrench them in the border and permit only negative effectiveness. Like watchdogs, they can stop people from doing some bad things. If they are wanted to do more, they would have to be organized differently.

The relation between social organization and values and beliefs can be demonstrated by an impressionistic exercise in grid/group analysis.[15] This is a way of checking characteristics of social organization with features of the beliefs and values of the people who are keeping the form of organization alive. *Group* means the outside boundary that people have erected between themselves and the outside world. *Grid* means all the other social distinctions and delegations of authority that they use to limit how people behave to one another. A society organized by hierarchy would have many group-encircling and group-identifying regulations plus many grid constraints on how to act. An individualist society would leave to individuals maximum freedom to negotiate with each other, so it would have no effective group boundaries and no insulating constraints on private dealings. A sectarian society would be recognizable by strong barriers identifying and separating the community from nonmembers, but it would be so egalitarian that it would have no leaders and no rules of precedence or protocol telling people how to behave. The distinctions are relative to some norm in some particular activity in some particular place and period. When this analysis is carefully applied, it shows up consistent patterns of shared values and beliefs, which are part of the everyday justifications sustaining each type of organization.

We can use this form of cultural analysis to compare some of the public-interest groups that mobilize concern for the environment and for the dangers of new technology. First we decide on indicators for group, then for grid; then we rank the organizations in question. We predict that a low score for grid and a high score for group will be more associated with sectarian cultural values. These are as follows. Objectives of the organization will be explicitly global in range, not local. They will explicitly include regenerating moral fervor. They will include counteracting a global conspiracy of evil. Members will expect to achieve their ends by small-scale organization. Their values will be against big technology, big industry, as well as big organization. They will expect and be on guard against infiltration from without. They will invoke the purity of the movement as a prime value. They will be apt to make symbolic statements of their rejection of the larger society and especially its technology, as by a preference for hand-loomed clothing, hand-thrown pottery, vegetable foods and dyes.

The comparison above of the Sierra Club with FOE already demonstrates the relation between the hierarchy and the sect and their respective cultural values. To carry the exercise further we can recall the history of the antinuclear movement in the United States to indicate the grid/group differences between the local intervener groups and the direct-action groups.

Until the làte 1960s antinuclear activity was almost exclusively concerned with campaigning against nuclear bombs. Protests against nuclear power were limited to a few, local, poorly organized efforts to stop particular projects. However, by the beginning of the 1970s there was a proliferation of local protest groups responding to the rapid expansion of the nuclear power program planned in response to the mounting costs of imported energy.

These organizations were initially formed by people who, living next to a proposed reactor site, were very concerned with the safety aspects of atomic power. They feared catastrophic accidents and also the effects of continued exposure to small doses of radiation. The organizers were mainly housewives, professionals, and retired people, often with a history of community involvement. Their activities primarily consisted of lobbying local and state politicians, intervening at hearings of the Nuclear Regulatory Commission or its predecessor, the Atomic Energy Commission, and initiating litigation to prevent such things as compulsory purchase of property and change of land use. Most of these local intervener groups had little formal structure and no requirements for membership. But as local groups increased their efforts to intervene in reactor licensing and to influence politicians and educate their neighbors, coalitions of groups began to form on a regional level. Doctors and scientists who had studied the problems of nuclear power and radiation, and lawyers, lobbyists, and community activists with special expertise in antinuclear issues, worked with a much larger number of local groups and helped to coordinate their activities. One such state-wide coalition was the Environmental Coalition on Nuclear Power (ECNP) described by Judith Johnsrud.[16] This coalition was brought together in 1970 for the purpose of providing a unified opposition at a hearing before the state legislature in Pennsylvania. In its ten years of existence, the organization has achieved several successes. Most notably, in 1975 the coalition managed to defeat the proposed development in Pennsylvania of several energy parks (concentrations of several power plants at one site) through a combination of legal and political activities.

The ECNP is one of the most active coalitions of local intervener groups. It illustrates the development of small, isolated
intervener groups opposing a local power plant, into formal
coalitions with common strategies opposing nuclear power in
an entire region.

The local intervener groups have a very high concentration
of middle-age and middle and upper class members. Their
motives for joining tend to be concern about property value,
noise pollution, general community impact, and reactor
safety. Most members of local intervener groups live within a
few miles of the plant they are fighting, and since most proposed reactors are sited in rural areas, most local interveners
live in small towns. The relative absence of the working class
and younger people from these groups may of course partially
be explained by the fact that in order to participate in legal
action, it is necessary to have both time and money. The proceedings are often demanding, lengthy, and specialized and
are usually carried on during the day. Unlike the direct-action
alliances, the localized concerns of most members of the intervener groups make it unlikely that the absence of working people would be a matter of great concern. Their limited aim is to
prevent nuclear power plants from being built in their back-
yards. They do not intend to democratize society.

As regional coalitions gained strength, some of them
attempted to forge national networks of antinuclear groups. In
1974 Ralph Nader called a citizens' conference that spawned a
network of national watchdog groups called Critical Mass.
Local and regional efforts, however, remain fairly isolated
both from one another and from the professional organizations
that concentrate on specific problems, such as nuclear waste
disposal. They are organized with a few specialized staff members, active directors and, perhaps, a national paper-membership. This paper-membership may well include individuals
from local intervener groups, and the national lobby organizations may well coordinate activities with groups expressing
opposition in local licensing procedures.

By the mid-1970s a growing number of nuclear power opponents had become impatient with opposition through litigation. Despite the occasional successes of the intervener coalitions, the nuclear regulatory agencies were seen as too heavily biased in favor of nuclear development for the intervention process to be effective. From the nuclear industry's viewpoint, government regulation may have held back the development of nuclear power, but many opponents felt that reliance on government regulation alone would never stop the expansion of nuclear power.

At this stage a series of direct-action organizations appeared, the Clamshell Alliance in New England, the Abalone Alliance in California, the Crabshell Alliance in Washington, the Catfish Alliance of the southern states, and others. The first major organization for direct action was formed in 1976 to oppose the construction of the nuclear power plant at Seabrook, New Hampshire. The license for this reactor had been granted despite opposition from *ad hoc* local groups, the Audubon Society, and the Society for the Protection of New Hampshire Forests. The granting of this license provoked the formation of the Clamshell Alliance as a coalition of twenty intervener, environmental, and new antinuclear groups dedicated to reversing the decision through direct action, including leaflets, petitions, alternative energy rallies and fairs, and nonviolent civil disobedience.

Since 1976 the Clamshell Alliance has coordinated several demonstrations and attempted occupations of nuclear sites. Clamshell focused its activities on resisting the construction of the Seabrook nuclear power plant. However, it emphasized that its opposition to Seabrook was merely a means of fighting nuclear power in general. According to its "Declaration of Nuclear Resistance," "A nuclear power plant at Seabrook, New Hampshire would lock our region into a suicidal path. As an affiliation of a wide range of groups and individuals, the Clamshell Alliance is unalterably opposed to the construction of this and any other nuclear power plant."[17] Action at Seabrook is a means of stopping this and any other nuclear power plant and of furthering the Alliance's overall demands, which include:

1. That not one more cent be spent on nuclear power reactors or nuclear weapons. . . .
2. That our energy policy be focused on developing and implementing clean and renewable sources of energy. . . .
3. That all people who lose jobs through the cancellation of nuclear construction, operation or weapons production be offered retraining and jobs in the natural energy field at decent, union-level wages.
4. That the supply of energy should in all cases be controlled by the people. . . .[18]

Clamshell itself has now grown to include over ninety member organizations. These alliances are strongly decentralized, with very different capabilities in terms of resources, sophistication, and size. But they all share a commitment to direct action, internal democracy, and major social reform. They differentiate themselves from the local intervener groups by being explicitly opposed to the system within which the latter are content to work.

The members of direct-action groups are usually younger than the local interveners. They tend to be white and, occupationally, few are involved in commerce, either as workers or managers. They are less often the immediate neighbors of a reactor site. Alan Sharaf notes that whereas three-quarters of the members of local intervener groups live within ten miles of the proposed nuclear power site, of the 1,414 demonstrators arrested during one major protest at Seabrook in 1977, only one-sixth were residents of New Hampshire, and only one-fifth of these lived within ten miles of the site.[19] Many of the major figures of the direct-action coalitions differ from the membership at large. Whereas most of the rank and file may be in their twenties, many of their leaders are in their thirties and were active in the antiwar movement. Unlike the local intervener groups, the direct-action alliances are constantly trying to expand the base of their membership. Members of the Clamshell Alliance see the absence of working-class support as a major obstacle facing the antinuclear movement (not least because the regional construction trade councils have been among the Alliance's chief antagonists).

First we note the organizational differences between the two types of movement. The local intervener groups do not have an overriding concern with democracy. Because many of the groups are organized on an *ad hoc* basis, the decisions are made by those who have the time and energy to attend meetings and to carry them out. Decisions may be made by simple majority on a show of hands. The interveners' indignation over violation of democracy is focused on decisions to build reactors without consultation with local residents.

By contrast, the meetings of the direct-action alliances lack even a chair. The preference is for a rotating facilitator whose job is to summarize what has been done and to make sure that the meeting reflects the ideas of everyone without moving policy in any particular direction. The facilitator has no special powers and cannot, for example, select an agenda or rule on procedures regarding how decisions should be made. One of the aims of this egalitarian mechanism is to prevent individuals coming to the fore and acting as spokespersons for the entire movement. Members of direct-action alliances are particularly suspicious of media-created superstars, whether from the entertainment or political world, who may be seen by the general public as leaders of the antinuclear movement. Many direct-action groups have a history of acrimonious confrontation with antinuclear politicians, such as Edmund Brown, Jr., because they feel that the support of any politician (even a public opponent of nuclear energy) implies an acceptance of the political system of larger society, as well as an espousal of leadership and hierarchy. An opponent of allowing Governor Brown to address an Abalone Alliance rally in 1979 protested:

The Abalone Alliance was formed as a direct action organization. It is based, as I understand it, on the acknowledgement that the forces which support nuclear power have enough of a stranglehold on the rest of economic and political life to protect their interests against challenges that confine themselves to the electoral, judicial or regulatory arenas. Direct action is organized activity that confronts the interests of the ruling class outside the manipulable forms of false democracy. Providing platforms for candidates for elective office is antithetical to its spirit.[20]

Both the extreme egalitarianism and the close-knit, small-scale organization of the direct activists are manifest in their affinity groups.

Perhaps the greatest strength of the Clamshell Alliance and the score of other regional alliances modeled on it has been the decentralized and participatory organizational structure borrowed from the Iberian Anarchist Federation of pre-Civil War Spain. Decisions are reached by consensus and are supposed to rest in "affinity groups," usually composed of ten to twenty members who share a common geographical or other affiliation. These are meant to be autonomous communal units that serve as catalysts for the initiative and consciousness of the movement.[21]

These groups are formed during the nonviolence training which is required by direct activists in preparation for large demonstrations. Through these groups an alliance can plan activities with thousands of participants and still retain a small-group, communal structure. Each participant is given an equal voice in group decision making. Affinity groups are expected to make specific plans for their role in any occupation of a reactor site. They may designate supporters who would not participate in the action but would do such things as bring supplies or coordinate legal defense. During the action, the affinity group is expected to stay together, make and execute plans together, and keep its members calm. Ideally they provide a means of dividing labor without recourse to leaders. Since most tasks are done separately by each affinity group, work can be divided among the members according to individual inclination.

The affinity group plays its part in the decision-making process of the whole alliance during a demonstration by designating a spokesperson (or *spoke,* as in the connecting links of a wheel) to represent the opinions of his or her group at meetings of decision-making bodies. The spoke is not an empowered representative and must report back to the affinity group before reaching new decisions. This method of decision making through consensus is enormously time consuming, especially when representatives need to run back and forth between

groups and meetings. Despite assurances that differences will
be worked out and an acceptable agreement will be reached,
individuals or groups can block consensus; and if holdouts
happen often enough, decisions are simply not made.

> When there were few people involved in the Abalone Alliance it was
> strengthening to work closely together, to agree on strategy, tactics
> and campaigns. Now, when the number of participants is much
> larger, this sort of complete agreement can be to our disadvantage.
>   It becomes much harder to reach agreement when more people
> are involved. Attempting to get hundreds of people to reach consen-
> sus is usually exhausting and often impossible.[22]

It is not uncommon to hear of meetings in which participants
cannot reach agreement or in which they spend hours discuss-
ing procedural questions. But for most groups these delays are
fully justifiable provided egalitarianism is maintained. As
among the Amish, each man is a priest; in San Francisco's
People Against Nuclear Power, each is a leader.

A contributor to *It's About Times* explains, "Our strength
springs from the nature of our movement. A decentralized
movement provides a strong foundation that can't be shaken
by attacks from society's 'top.' We are our own leaders and
there are simply too many of us with too many good ideas for
them to counter and manipulate us in their normal manner."[23]
More frankly, Betsy Taylor recognizes, "There's a kind of par-
anoia about people taking leadership. . . . Anybody claiming
leadership runs into problems in this movement because there
just isn't anybody who is in a position of leading it. . . . In some
places it's just torn groups apart because if you try to take initiative and do something positive you're criticized for tying to
seize power."[24]

One of the purposes of the direct activists' carefully maintained, small-unit structure is to avoid major disagreement
within the alliance. When a group gets too large to make decisions communally, it is supposed to divide into component
parts. Rather than growing until a major disagreement splits
the organization apart, many alliances have, like the Hutter-

ites, incorporated splits into their organizational structure. This mechanism has been largely successful in preventing major ideological rifts in direct-action alliances. Although they have often been paralyzed by the inability of member units to agree on a particular course of action, this has rarely led to the establishment of competing splinter groups. The independent action of local groups does not challenge the entire organization; they are expected to act on their own.

To summarize, whereas action groups have strict rules about how decisions are to be made and how the organization is to be administered, these rules are designed to prevent hierarchical-type leaders from taking control and to provide for the resolution of disputes in the absence of authority. In contrast, local intervener groups have a much less formal view of their internal structures. They are organized as groups of equals because they join the movement through their friends and neighbors. A formal structure is generally deemed unnecessary. Most local intervener groups value flexibility and speedy action. Elaborate rules and procedures designed to maintain absolute equality would hamper them. Leaders can and do emerge, and decisions are made by individuals or elites. Individuals appropriate roles as public representatives. Almost all direct-action groups would consider a decision made in ten hours through consensus infinitely preferable to the same one made in ten minutes by a small group of leaders. Clearly, the activist groups conform more closely to the organizational practice of sects. Their strong barriers against the outside world are formed on the judgment that it is a waste of time to use legal and political processes to negotiate with central institutions or to participate in Nuclear Regulatory Committee hearings.

The strength of a group depends for one thing on how clearly members can be identified. The activists' test of membership is the stringent one of willingness to participate in direct action on a face-to-face basis. Let us compare the Clamshell Alliance and the ECNP. Both encourage a periphery of supporters who are sympathetic to the cause, attend meetings, or write letters of protest without being involved in direct action or legal intervention. This periphery protects members from directly experiencing hostile attitudes and insulates the group from the world at large. Along the group dimension we can further distinguish the Clamshell Alliance from the ECNP. The latter is organized on a central core of committed local members organizing meetings on an *ad hoc* basis, and people freely enter or leave the core; by contrast the membership of a Clamshell affinity group is supposed to keep the same personnel, an organization core of between five to thirty members. Each affinity group is further bounded off by its self-sufficiency: it is supposed to be able to perform for itself all its necessary functions in any occupation or demonstration. So we give the Clamshell Alliance a higher score for group boundedness than the ECNP.

On the grid assessment, the Clamshell Alliance comes up with a much lower score than the ECNP. It recognizes no leaders and no officers.

The Clam is supposed to be leaderless, but of course it isn't. Carleton Eldredge, the rather unpredictable district attorney of Rockingham County, has had to deal with the organization on several occasions, and he says, "The leaders resist identifying themselves, but when they want something, the same people show up to talk to you." . . . The leaders, naturally, are the people who do most of the work between occupations. . . . If they tend to hide in the crowd, it is not to outfox officials such as Eldredge but to avoid criticism from other Clams. Sam Lovejoy, the most obvious leader, was in deep hiding; he didn't even come to Seabrook this time.[27]

The *de facto* leader keeps a very low profile. He acts more as a guru or a *primus inter pares,* on the basis of perhaps a little more experience, a way with words, or a flair for tactics; but all the Alliance's rules pertaining to leadership are designed to prevent the emergence of individual leaders. While the ECNP also rejects formal leadership in the sense of elected officers, it lacks rules which are deliberately designed to prevent the emergence of leaders. Leaders of intervener groups tend to be entrepreneurial individuals who take on the leading roles in promoting local opposition to nuclear plants. Hence the ECNP rates higher on the grid dimension than the strictly egalitarian Clamshell Alliance.

This crude typification of differences in organization corresponds to a striking difference in cultural bias. The local intervener groups that constitute the ECNP are concerned about safety and noise during construction, the effects on the community of locating a nuclear plant close by, and all the possible economic and social changes, as well as the potential nuclear dangers to the community and the effects that the perception of such danger might have on such things as property values. The ECNP accepts the established legal channels as appropriate for fighting the antinuclear battle. Its democratic concern is that the existing system is not working properly insofar as local residents do not have an adequate say in the siting of nuclear reactors. They do not, however, reject the existing social system as unworkable or fundamentally unjust. They have a precise target, to prevent one or another nuclear power station from being built. Clamshell places the social values of a nonnuclear society well to the fore of their campaign. In the pursuit of this democratic vision, the activist groups feel the need to bring workers and minorities into the struggle for reform.

There is . . . a growing realization that to be truly effective the antinuclear movement will have to build coalitions with organized labor. On this point there is still a lack of clarity as to how the vision of a world without nuclear power plants and weapons translates into a specific strategy that includes labor as a natural ally.[26]

Most members of direct-action alliances joined because of their opposition to nuclear power, both as a technology and as the manifestation of undemocratic unresponsiveness to individual needs within American society. Nuclear power is a capital-intensive and highly centralized industry which concentrates control of energy in the hands of the corporate leaders. Their concern for democracy is exhibited in almost every

aspect of their organization and activity. Their aims include
reforming society and developing democratically controlled,
localized sources of energy. "The politics of anti-nuclear protest constitute one of the most potentially revolutionary forces
in contemporary America. Not only because of its commitments in facing the question of energy development under
capitalism, but in the *very way* the movement has *organized
itself,* and its critique of issues such as leadership and power."[27]
The Clamshell Alliance views all economic and social ills as
stemming from the distribution of energy in favor of large corporate and governmental interests. Their aim in blocking
nuclear power is not merely to safeguard themselves from the
possibilities of exposure to hazardous radiation but to break
the stranglehold which they consider such interests have on
society. The extreme egalitarianism of their own organization
is seen as a model for future world government. Thus the
Clamshell Alliance concentrates all social, economic, and political issues into the nuclear debate. And according to Harvey
Wasserman, one of the founders of the Clamshell Alliance and
a major speaker for the movement:

At its core, the nuclear issue is a confrontation between corporate,
technocratic domination and decentralized, community independence. The choice is closely linked to a broad spectrum of issues — to
unemployment and high electric rates, to exploitation of Third
World people and resources, to the plagues of nuclear armaments,
environmental chaos, and our soaring cancer rates.[28]

Once again we observe the trend for various issues to coagulate
into one global stand against evil in all its forms. This illustrates well the sectarian features of the cultural change we
have been examining.

To our explanation of cultural bias, we now have added a
method for identifying the changes in organization that go
along with changes in cultural values. The futher the organization is toward border values, the stronger we find the social
indicators for group membership and the weaker those for grid
distinctions. With more fieldwork we could put more precise

measures upon the conditions of voluntary organizations that cause them to erect a boundary against the world and to invoke dangers from technology.[29] We claim that the success of the ecology movement in this country represents a shift of the more vocal parts of American life towards the border. We still have not explained how that shift came about or what maintains it. Until we answer the question of why America is more passionately involved than any other Western nation in the debate about risks to nature, we cannot explain what has been happening here.

VIII

America Is A Border Country

Why did sectarian forces grow so much stronger in America in the mid-1960s? It is not easy to explain why significant events occurred at a particular point in time. There are general historical factors operating throughout American history. There are medium-range factors, closer to the time in question, that facilitate the emergence of certain patterns of behavior. And there are short-term factors predisposing the events to occur when they do. Sectarianism, we contend, has always had some strength in America. Its potential has increased because of widespread changes in education, industry, and political mobilization that manifested themselves in mid-century; and its recent successes were gained because of its ability to make use of new political technology in the midst of other contemporaneous challenges to trust in American institutions.

GENERAL HISTORICAL FACTORS

Since the current set of public fears so closely corresponds to the sectarian view of the world, we recall the fertility of the American social scene for cultivating sectarian types of organization. The reader familiar with American history will recognize that our interpretation on this point is not idiosyncratic but travels well-worn paths. As David Vogel says:

> In fact, the political perspective that informs the public-interest movement is not at all peculiar to the last decade; it is deeply rooted in the American political tradition. Its key elements—the importance of individual initiative, the fear of public authority, the value of increased political competition, an uneasiness with majoritarian democracy, the fascination with law and legal procedures, the emphasis on voluntary organizations—all can be found in both Hartz and de Tocqueville.[1]

Among the early settlers of America, as every schoolboy knows, were communities of people who came to avoid religious persecution. America was their wilderness to which they fled from the intolerance of the established churches. Once arrived, they often manifested the same degree of intolerance toward those who disagreed with them, leading to new splits and migrations. The apocalyptic character of these religious movements (catastrophe always being around the corner) as well as their millennialism (opening up glorious vistas after mankind shall have been liberated from evil institutions) has been fully recorded. So has the fear of subversion by invisible forces that enter the body politic unseen, like Satan's minions. Anyone who lived through the 1950s in the United States recognized the resemblance between the Puritan's fear of witchcraft and Senator Joseph McCarthy's allegations that the State Department had been penetrated by the invisible forces of International Communism tied to evil forces in Moscow.

In America there was never a question of a border because states existed before there was a nation. Always the question was whether there would be a center. Compared to the people of other industrial nations, Americans have been the least concerned about weakness at the center. The Articles of Confederation created a center so weak it could not stand. Instead of shoring up the system with an all-powerful center, the framers of the Constitution equivocated, giving it coercive authority over individuals while restraining its possible excesses.

Throughout American history, concern over the weakness of central authority has alternated with fear it would grow too strong. Yet even when the desire for a strong central authority is high in America, it is low on the scale of other large, industrial democracies.

There is plenty of resonance in early American political life with a sectarian culture. Recall the debates during the constitutional convention and in *The Federalist Papers* on the evils of faction. Defining a faction as composed of people sharing common aims and acting adversely to the interests of others, James Madison (in the justly famous tenth number of the *Federalist*) sought to design a constitutional structure that would tame this wild and passionate beast. The people's preferences were to be refined through successive stages. One technique would be to vary electorates for different offices. The separation of powers and the system of checks and balances would use the ambition of one set of officials to counter that of the others. The substantial size of the republic, then thought to prohibit popular government, would prevent factions from getting together to suppress others. This intricate Newtonian machinery of balancing forces, to be sure, is not sectarian. It recalls that, from the outset, factionalism has been recognized as a force that threatens strong central government. *Curing the Mischiefs of Faction,*[2] as Austin Ranney has titled his elegant book, has been a major preoccupation of American politics.

Accusations of secret, malign influence have been perennial. When public participation in politics increased, the congressional caucus for choosing presidential candidates was attacked as a conspiratorial cabal, and it was overturned in favor of the more participatory presidential nominating convention. This developmental trend toward wider public participation was foreseen by Alexis de Tocqueville in his celebration of the virtues—energy, originality, diversity—and the vices—rashness, restlessness, divisiveness—of egalitarian organizations.[3]

"The public-interest movement," David Vogel writes, ". . . represents a historically conditioned response to the problems posed for the American politics by the rise of the large business corporation in the latter third of the nineteenth century."[4] The Progressive era ushered in two complementary movements — increased public participation in politics and protection of the environment against industrial exploitation.[5] On the political side, national nominating conventions were made more participatory by introducing presidential primaries. And an effort was made to make government more responsive through the initiative (passing legislation or constitutional amendments by popular ballot) and the recall (turning public officials out of office before their terms were over). Both measures reveal distrust of large organizations (private and public) and a preference for more open politics. On the environmental side, the end of the frontier brought a new fear: the United States was running out of wilderness. Public policy created vast regions of national, state, county, local, and regional parks. Public boundaries separated the pure land that would remain undeveloped and uncontaminated from that which would be subject to commercial exploitation.

The two unifying institutions of American national politics are the political parties and the presidency. We see them rise and fall as the problems faced by the nation change. The economic depression of the 1930s, the Second World War, and the fear of international communism strengthened central institutions and the role of government. As the threat appeared to be external or to require the refurbishing of economic productivity, defense of the system was the order of the day. By the mid-1960s, however, signs of older preoccupations appeared. A revival of political sectarianism became evident. James Q. Wilson wrote about *The Amateur Democrat*[6] who replaces social and employment ties to party with a strong orientation to particular issues. Amateurs of this type are unwilling to let professional party officials and public office holders decide these matters by themselves.

In the 1964 and 1968 elections, sectarian integrity was idealized in both parties. Purity was an obsession. Thus, at the
Republican nominating convention of 1964, the supporters of
presidential aspirant Barry Goldwater referred to his best
quality as "moral integrity," for "he does not compromise." As
one said, memorializing the idea of politics as opposition, "I
think everything ought to be an issue. . . ."[7] At the 1968 Democratic Party convention, supporters of Eugene S. McCarthy
used youth as their symbol of uncorrupted integrity. They
wanted "a truly representative party that isn't controlled by the
people at the top or by men with money." They believed that
"Gene is doing this for us. He'll never give away our policies
and our ideals. He won't betray us." They were "for Gene . . .
because he isn't a politician."[8] There was growing conflict between the roles of "purists" and "politicians," the latter seeking
to win elections by pleasing voters and the former, by purity
and integrity, remaining true to their policy convictions
regardless of the electoral outcome.

One could hardly invent a series of actions to show sectarian
influence more clearly than those that have recently occurred.
The presidential nominating conventions have been taken over
by a proliferation of primaries, acting against the party
"bosses" and the old "smoke-filled rooms" where these wheelers
and dealers allegedly used to decide the fate of the nation. If,
as the texts say, the main function of a political party is to
nominate candidates for office, there is not much function
left. Even more evocative of sectarian attempts to achieve
equality are the rules of the national Democratic Party requiring the most precise percentages of blacks, Hispanics, youth,
women, and other ethnic and biological groups to receive rep-
resentation in proportion to their numbers.[9]

Divisions within the so-called ruling class have been a feature of American politics from its earliest days. The American
revolution, we must not forget, pitted a colonial against an
imperial establishment, one form of hierarchy against another.
After the revolution, when popular currents in state legisla-
tures threatened to debase the currency, and with it social

order, the former revolutionary elites coalesced to create the Constitution. Just as democracy is correctly called the institutionalization of conflict, so a government that is based on popular consent encourages elites to compete. This may be, but is not necessarily, "me-too-ism." Amid the competing claims for power, as the Progressive movement showed, are serious charges that the regime in power is corrupt, incompetent, boss-ridden, and run by secret forces. To this extent, the opposition within the establishment may sound sectarian, just because it is in opposition. But its program was really hierarchical. The Progressives held themselves out as the apostles of efficiency, from Taylor's assembly-line work methods, to nonpartisan civil service, to executive budgets, to stewardship of the land by scientifically trained experts. They sought what Andrew McFarland called civic balance, in which one form of big organization, the government, is called on to control another, big business.[10]

It was the Populists who did not wish to reform but to replace the existing establishment. The Populists did not wish to modify markets by planning, as the Progressives did, but to reject the price system as fatally flawed. The Populists were market rejectors on grounds that markets inculcated vicious social principles — social coercion and economic inequality.

Opposition to existing institutions in the United States has historically had two cultural sources — hierarchy and sectarianism. The hierarchical source stands ready to replace the existing elite with a worthier administration. The sectarian source challenges authority itself without necessarily seeking or being able to replace it. According to the historical record, sectarianism has evidently been weaker. Why, then, has it grown stronger in recent times?

MEDIUM-RANGE FACTORS

It is not enough to say that from the very beginning the American cultural climate has been conducive to sectarianism. The beginning was a long time ago. Something has happened in the last twenty years to favor its reemergence.

At the immediate level of self-interest there are always explanations that fit the facts about certain groups. Just as an increasing concern over national defense favors certain types of industry, so does concern over safety help other organizations, including labor unions, who can get government to pay for increasing the safety of its members or to compensate them for the damage they do suffer (for example, from black lung disease). Leaders looking for positions may discover the environment as their predecessors discovered unions. Being comfortable but not rich, environmentalists may welcome using other people's money to keep competitors away from the wilderness. Still, explaining the popularity of a trend by saying it attracted people who made it popular leaves something lacking.

According to Joseph Schumpeter, the preeminent theorist of the demise of individualism through its own success, the institutionalization of innovation in capitalism breeds the very qualities—skepticism, criticism, leisure—that will corrode its social structure. As the economy created wealth, Schumpeter argued, it would also make room for intellectuals who would hate the crudities and resist the discipline of the system that spawned them. To sum up in his own words,

capitalism stands its trial before judges who have the sentence of death in their pockets.... Secular improvement that is taken for granted and coupled with individual insecurity that is acutely resented is of course the best recipe for breeding social unrest....
Nevertheless, neither the opportunity of attack nor real or fancied grievances are in themselves sufficient to produce, however strongly they may favor, the emergence of active hostility against a social order. For such an atmosphere to develop it is necessary that there be groups to whose interest it is to work up and organize resentment, to nurse it, to voice it and to lead it.[11]

What happened in the decades preceding the 1960s, we ask, that predisposed certain people toward such social criticism?

Three differences distinguished the United States from other democracies in the period after World War II. First, it had a far larger proportion of its population in higher education; second, it had a significant racial minority; and third, that minority came to political consciousness at the same time as the children of its majority were elbowing each other out of the way in graduate school. Looking back to the 1960s and 1970s we see three influences on the public interest movement: from the economy, availability; from the polity, opportunity; from history, exemplars of how to organize protest movements.

To understand further why this contemporary movement of social concern began earlier and with greater strength in America than in Europe, first consider the historical developments in the economy. While the entire West showed economic growth after the Second World War, expansion was uneven, but America was well in the lead. Starting from a higher economic base, the absolute increments of growth were much larger in America than elsewhere. Given the relative absence of class barriers, imbued with equality of opportunity, American higher education exploded in size. By the mid-1960s, most high school graduates went to a college or university. The proportion of college-age students enrolled in higher education was from two to ten times the levels in Western Europe and Japan. This was the result of real affluence.

The United States produced more educated people than could be absorbed in industry; their talents tended to mobilize words and people. As the size of government expanded with the size of the economy, positions were created for research program managers and evaluators. Vast new cadres of employees in the arts, social sciences, and humanities generally, as well as in government, were set apart from those involved with industrial production. The economy shifted its weight toward the service sector.[12] A larger proportion of the population of working age was disengaged from the production process than had been before. The economic boom and the educational boom together produced a cohort of articulate, critical people with no commitment to commerce and industry. The entry of enormous numbers of young people into higher education kept them outside the mainstream of American economic life while they were in school, and when they came out of school most new jobs opened up in service industries.

The shift to service industries makes room for educated people of the border. Though on the average they work in smaller units than do their peers in production, service intellectuals are less disposed to suffer subordination to hierarchy. After all, their level of formal education is often as high as or higher than the old captains of industry, who had such a large voice in making decisions affecting other people. Where before, engaged in production, educated people could see why collective constraint might be necessary, working in the service sector suggests such subordination is unnecessary. Removed from the "firing line," not having to meet the "bottom line," the boundary between service and production becomes one between border and center. The more the means of production are ideas rather than things, the less the hierarchical organization of production appears essential.

Their situation may well be comparable to that of the Russian intelligentsia. The separation between the educated and the ordinary people (the educated often spoke French at home rather than Russian) began when Peter the Great sought to modernize his country by sending young men to the West, bringing them back to become the new leaders of his feudal nation. This social separation was reemphasized in the period from the emancipation of the serfs in 1861 to the Bolshevik Revolution of 1918. Although this critical intelligentsia had high social and economic status, it cut itself off from the centers of society, equally from the then-dominant political collectivism as from the growing entrepreneurial economic individualism.[13] The rise of that cadre, with relatively high income and education but with no direct relationship to economic production, has been celebrated in literature and its influence fiercely debated. Some lived dilettantish lives, squandering their inheritances. Others advocated a return to the people on the land, often to discover that the peasants they came to help did not want any such return. Still others organized reformist or revolutionary movements, paying for their protest by exile, death, or obscurity. Since the United States is already industrialized, however, its situation requires a more specific explanation.[14]

Given the hierarchical structure of the processes of production, people who take part in them should be expected to see fewer distant dangers than those of equivalent social and economic standing who do not. Since perceptions of environmental impurities form part of a critique of the existing social system, we would expect people who stand outside industrial society to be more concerned about risk from pollution. It is not only that people who take part in production feel more kindly about its processes but that their fortunes are tied to those of the central society. Its failures are theirs and so are its successes. Threats to the economy or to the polity endanger their core concerns. If the economy does not keep growing, the promises of past generations to the present and of the present to the future, both justifying the sacrifices imposed by hierarchies, cannot be kept.

Stephen Cotgrove and his colleagues at Bath University in England have sampled the views of members of Friends of the Earth and the Conservative Society and have taken another sample from *Business Who's Who* and *Who's Who in Engineering*. They asked whether their respondents thought environmental problems were extremely serious, hardly serious at all or someplace in between. They then subsampled those who were most worried (calling them catastrophists) and those who were hopeful for future prosperity (calling them cornucopians). The cornucopians were more in favor of economic growth in industrial society and accorded more deference to experts. The catastrophists were anti-industrial, denigrated economic growth, and favored an enhanced sense of belonging to a community. Cornucopians and catastrophists have different social positions, but not on a simple class basis.

The cornucopians are typically in occupations which are central to the production process in industrial society. . . . Few catastrophists are in such jobs. The cornucopians are typically engineers, consultants, directors, managers, marketing and sales people, industrial scientists. The catastrophists are typically research scientists, academics, doctors, teachers, clergy, social workers, writers, actors and artists.[15]

It seems that those who get their living from industry trust the industrial process more than those who work in communications, teaching, and writing.

After World War II the Vietnam War shook the bases of central authority in America. In England the Suez crises and in France the Algerian crisis had similar but less pronounced effects. Although the United States was not defeated on its homeland, its traditional institutions bore the brunt of a dual failure — military and moral. The evidence of military loss appeared as retribution for the immoral institutions that had directed the fighting. The center was doubly delegitimized by fighting for a foreign regime that did not even espouse its own democratic values and by losing the fight. It was not so surprising, then, that the sectarian sermon was preached: the evil is at home, emanating from our own social system.

The Watergate affair, in which the head of the government disgraced himself and was forced to resign, did nothing to restore respect to the center. On the contrary, the evidence of a cover-up, complete with illicit break-ins, secret tapes, and clandestine meetings, could have been made to order for sectarian conspiracy theories.

No doubt there were excellent reasons for Americans to distrust large-scale military and governmental organizations. Among them, the Vietnam War, the Watergate affair, and the struggle over civil rights were enough to give anyone pause. No doubt these episodes strengthened negative feelings about American government and society. There is considerable evidence that people who were in their teens and twenties from the mid-sixties to mid-seventies thought environmental problems more serious than older or younger people.[16] In a nice turn around, Malkis and Malkis argue that having disposed of the military half of the "military-industrial complex," the youth movement of that era was turning its attention to the industrial half.[17]

The antipollution movements benefited from an extraordinary exemplar. Political instruction came about through imitating the tactics of the civil rights movement. Let us begin with what Gunnar Myrdal properly called *An American Dilemma*.[18] Black people were always a bone lodged in the throat of American individualism. They couldn't be swallowed whole and the American value system could not breathe freely with them stuck in a peculiar place. Indeed, the civil rights movement, through which a measure of civil and political equality was achieved, earned an honorific place in American life because it sought to redress wrongs in the name of a central value of American individualism — equality before the law. It was good against evil, a modern morality play in which a minority carried the creed. Everything connected with the civil rights movement, therefore, became ennobled, including its tactics — nonviolent protest, nonnegotiable demands (how could you negotiate the birthright of every American?), and due process of law. Increased political participation, use of government to achieve group gains, use of lawsuits to claim rights, insistence that rules and regulations be followed punctiliously as a means of enforcing compliance — these procedural reforms achieved an almost hallowed status by association.

Gary Orfield, in *Congress and Social Change,* attributes the initiation of environmental legislation to Congress itself.[19] His views are persuasive. Andrew McFarland argues that politicians will always jump aboard a popular bandwagon[20] and, in the early 1970s, environmentalism was that. No doubt something would have been done. But the moralism of this legislation — setting standards that could not be met, using legal orders to enforce them, refusing to consider costs — was manifestly sectarian and may well have been influenced by the civil rights movement.

Had black people been allowed to exercise the rights of

other Americans earlier, it is possible they would have accepted the American way as did voluntary immigrant groups, absorbing the value system in its entirety, hook, line, and sinker. Had that happened, the demand for equality would have been a demand for equality of opportunity as in an individualist platform, not equality of results as in sectarianism.

The struggle for civil rights temporarily submerged the potential conflict between the two principles. All that black Americans needed, some thought, was an equal chance. When experience revealed that decades of deprivation had taken their toll, so that those disadvantaged before needed more than an equal chance now, the demands shifted to equal results for black people as a group. It was no longer enough to be allowed to run in the race; it became necessary for a proportionate number of blacks to win. Racial quotas, which had been anathema, became acceptable. From this shift in the paradigm of equality flowed a sequence of important consequences. First, white, liberal support split into factions, one favoring "opportunity" and one favoring "results." Second, civil rights groups such as the Congress of Racial Equality (CORE) and the Student Nonviolent Coordinating Committee (SNCC),[21] rejected white leadership. Thus a cadre of white activists, accustomed to leadership and trained to represent deprived groups, was left out of work and free to lead the fight against risks perpetrated by giant corporations and big government on the public at large.[22] The major manifestation of their leadership became the public interest group.

SHORT-TERM FACTORS

"A public interest group," according to Jeffrey Berry, "is one that seeks a collective good, the achievement of which will not selectively and materially benefit the membership or activists of the organization."[23] Unlike farm or labor groups, for instance, the benefits they seek, such as cleaner air or open government, are for all citizens. Members may benefit, but presumably these benefits are shared. Immediately we know (see chapters VI and VII) that public interest groups must suffer all the difficulties of voluntary associations. They must keep mustering enthusiasm or their members will withdraw. The big-interest members will be blackmailed by the small-interest members. Thus, in order to retain membership, their organizational costs must be very low. They appear to be unable to organize to achieve a collective public good. Yet they do organize and achieve. Why? How?

Two things have appeared: one, mail-order memberships, a product of modern technology; the other, opportunities for support generated by big government. First we take up the communications technology, then the government.

The use of computerized mailing lists has permitted sectarian groups to tap sources of contributions from large numbers of people who do not participate directly in the groups' activities. This opportunity for vicarious participation has not only produced ready cash but has also simplified the task of leadership. Instead of satisfying an active membership that might make contradictory demands, only the top leadership need be considered. They are poorly paid, accepting low income as a sacrifice for their cause. Moving from one group to another, they reduce organization overhead by providing experienced lobbying at low cost.

The relation to government of the public interest groups is that they are regulated by the Internal Revenue Service; people who contribute to them are entitled to count these monies as tax-deductible. Where deductibility is inconvenient for the entire group, it often establishes a separate educational or litigation "arm." Without tax-deductibility, the survival of some of these groups would be in doubt. The trade-off is that they do not engage in overt lobbying. They do engage in educational activities, which may be a distinction without a difference.

The dual advantages of gaining material, financial support and of getting government to coerce other interests make modern forces of sectarianism extremely powerful. Instead of being subject to other people's rules, they impose, through government, an immense array of rules on their opponents. Many like to use the judiciary because "it epitomizes their ideal of public authority without public bureaucracy."[24] They get stronger as their enemies are made weaker. Direct help, in terms of grants for research and support for lawsuits, keeps the groups going. By requiring their presence at hearings and their voice in proceedings, the status of intervenor makes them more important.

The growth and financing of public interest law centers may serve to illustrate the importance of governmental support. These centers grew from fifteen in 1969 to 120 in 1980 and deal with poverty law as well as environmental law. Originally, they received substantial support from private foundations, which is now declining. Contributions from the general public make up about one-third of center budgets. Where does the rest come from? A seminar on "Financing Public Interest Advocacy," sponsored by the Center for Responsive Governance and the Interagency Council on Citizen Participation, reports:

> The federal government is now the leading contributor to public interest law, with 33 percent of total funds coming from this source. It appears to be taking up some of the slack left by decreasing dollars from foundations. Federal funds constitute the largest source of support for poverty centers (which include Legal Services national support projects), and provide an even greater share to groups representing minorities and disabled/handicapped persons. General public interest law firms, prisoner groups and environmental groups are also turning to the government as a potential source of funds. . . .
>
> The other form that government funding of public interest law has taken is direct grants by federal agencies to public interest centers or their clients for participation in particular agency proceedings.

Although the legal profession does not yet support these centers, "Attorneys' fees represent an increasingly significant source of income for centers. The courts are now beginning to award fees to prevailing plaintiffs generally at levels high enough to encourage lawyers to handle such cases."[25]

The federal government subsidizes most everyone's lobbying. Business gets tax-subsidized lobbying; membership in trade associations qualifies as a business expense. Public interest groups get postal subsidies, some government grants, and intervenor status. State and local government lobbies receive many grants for research. For groups that would otherwise lack a financial base, governmental subsidy means more than it would to others that are better endowed.

By this means the border actually gets the center to allocate funds for its border objectives. Sectarian groups have created new agencies, new antipollution and anticarcinogen laws requiring billions in corporate expenditures, and new processes, such as impact statements, adding up to institutionalized awareness of environmental and personal damage. In 1974, according to the Council of Environmental Quality, some nineteen government agencies spent over $6 billion on environmental purposes.[26] These developments materialized the very apotheosis of sectarian dreams.

The setup is superb for a small group of professional leaders in contact with a large, unorganized, compliant mail-order membership. On one side, leadership positions are multiplied without the usual constraints of voluntary group membership; on the other, demands on members are far less stringent than the full commitment of sects. Taken together as a statement of political economy, the costs of entry in influencing government (a few dollars per mail-order member) and of activity (lobbying and legal work) have been vastly reduced.

But where does the passionate commitment to the cause of public interest groups come from? In summing up the relationship to their work of employees of public interest lobbies, Berry says that "for the most part these people are zealots, and they derive a great deal of satisfaction from their jobs. In contrast to the more mildly committed private interest lobbyists, the public interest lobbyists are more likely to seek out the work they are doing, rather than merely 'drift' into it."[27]

In the division of responsibilities and powers within the top level of public interest groups, Berry's interviews suggest that staff was more important than board. Basically, this is also true in many corporations; boards ratify what management proposes unless and until there are moments of crisis. "For public interest groups," Berry tells us,

> advocacy choices must be understood in the context of the staff's domination and personalized decision making that characterizes so many of the organizations. . . . It is clear that the power to choose new issues on which to lobby rests in the hands of the staff members in most of the organizations. The men and women who run the public interest groups do not sit at the apex of large bureaucracies. Fifty-four percent of the Washington offices have three or fewer staff professionals, and 90% have 10 or less. Consequently, these groups, which ostensibly "speak for the people," do so through the voices of a very few.[28]

Though Berry is thinking that the leaders of public interest groups are not representative of their membership, we would observe that these leaders' groups are ideally suited for sectarian activity. They are small in size, work hard (both attributes that cut costs), do important things, and are kept together by an emphasis on how bad it is in the established society outside their groups. Were members to join government or work consistently within the organizations they criticize, we would expect them to attack one another for selling out.

The task of mustering enthusiasm, both for the full-time, paid staff and the part-time, mail-order membership of public interest groups, is accomplished by an evocative and artful choice of themes. It begins with their ability to get their self-designation accepted in public discourse and goes on to threaten all sorts of dire consequences that can be alleviated by a little extra effort or a small contribution.

The label "public interest group" is more than merely convenient; it is also flattering. It suggests that these groups are pure (their interests are public, open, and shared) in contrast to other groups presumed to be impure (behind their public advocacy lie their private interests). Each claims to place general public interests, such as health, safety, and proper procedure, above particular private interests. This elevation serves them well. At once they are able to disclaim selfish motives, such as direct pecuniary gain, while advancing policies to use public money upon what Inglehart would call their postmaterial preferences. Whether the seeking of power, status, leadership, and personal visibility belongs to a higher moral plane than seeking better wages and profits we do not judge; but on principle we challenge claims to extra holiness.

The political views of the border are predictably on the left. Around two-thirds of public interest activists identify with the Democratic party, compared to about 40 percent of the general public. When asked to place themselves on the usual political scale, about three-fourths of activists in public interest organizations saw themselves, in American terms, as liberal or radical.[29]

The rank and file are kept together by choosing the widest possible sectarian appeal — man's natural goodness, his corruption by big hierarchical organizations, and his redemption through a return to the natural, undifferentiated order of things. The common danger to human survival is recognized as coming from a technological attack on nature. We argue that voluntary associations choose to be panic-struck about dangers from technology rather than from threats to the economy or education because they serve their own moral purposes by focusing on dangers emanating from large organization rather than on dangers arising from inadequate investment, blundering foreign policy, or undereducation. By looking more closely at the inducements to membership in public interest groups, we shall see more clearly the attractions of attacking the center from the border.

What does the ordinary mail-order member get from these public interest groups that keep asking for contributions? After all, in Mancur Olson's terms, the benefits these groups seek are available to all; no one can be excluded from clean air or honest government. Why, then, do most people not become free riders, gaining the benefits but not paying the costs? A convincing answer is contributed by Robert C. Mitchell who argues

that these [member] contributions are compatible with behavior of the egoistic, rational, utility-maximizing kind because the cost is low, the potential cost of not contributing is high and the individual has imperfect information about the effectiveness of his or her contribution in obtaining the good or preventing the bad.[30]

The main distinction Mitchell makes is between public goods and public "bads," that is, bad things imposed on everyone whether they like it or not. Like what? Like the evils listed by environmental interest groups in their direct mail, fund-raising efforts:

According to the National Parks and Conservation Association, *"our National Parks are in danger"*;... the National Audubon Society warns against "sacrificing" our land, water, and air to appease the "furies of inflation"; the Environmental Defense Fund raises the "threat from poisoned air, water and food"; the Natural Resources Defense Council offers itself as an "inspired and effective approach to preserve a liveable world"; the Friends of the Earth remind us that [if we] "continue to pollute the air in our major cities... there will soon be no such thing as fresh air for us to breathe"; and the National Wildlife Federation seeks to meet "the crisis [of] the continued survival of man and wildlife on this fragile planet."...

Perhaps the most important factor which makes the disutility of environmental bads such an important motivating force for contributions to environmental lobbies is the fact that the bads have a very strong no-exit quality to them....

Jacques Cousteau is especially explicit about the importance of the no-exit factor in a 1978 fund-raising letter: "I beg you not to dismiss this possibility [of death of the oceans] as science fiction. The ocean can die, these horrors could happen. *And there would be no place to hide!*" (emphasis added).[31]

Under these threatening circumstances, from which there is no escape, a few dollars a year for survival may not appear to be too high a price to pay.

What Olson calls the inconsequentiality problem — would any one person's action make a difference? — has to be solved before it is worthwhile to contribute. Citing the disagreement among experts and the appeals to avoid ecological disaster, Mitchell concludes that individual persons may rationally wish to avoid the worst (minimize their maximum regret). Thus the sectarian strategy of telling people how bad it is in the outside world, when combined with technology that has drastically decreased the costs of organizing, explains the ability of certain public interest groups to attract and maintain contributing members.

Observing that these public interest groups make use of modern means of communication does not explain why they are so extraordinarily successful in comparison, let us say, to business interests. It is true that the new agencies and regulations cost government little in direct outlay, with much of the work being done through courts and most of the money being spent by private industry, presumably passed on as higher prices to consumers. Nonetheless, ability to raise modest amounts of money, to go to court, and to lobby in Washington would not in itself necessarily enable them to overcome the influence of much richer groups. Yet these lobbies fill the legislative landscape with major bills on water and air quality, environmental protection, occupational health and safety, automobile regulation, and so much more. The reaction against their successes by the administration of Republican President Ronald Reagan in 1981 is a testimony to how much they have achieved.

One difficulty in appreciating the power of environmental public interest groups lies in their deceptive lack of structure. Indeed their very headlessness is their structure. "Atoms were accepted as really 'real,'" Popper observes, "when they ceased to be 'atomic,' when they ceased to be indivisible bits of matter; when they acquired a structure."[32]

Hierarchies are easy to describe; nests of boxes make neat organizational charts. Sects without internal differentiation are simpler. The pyramid of power is diffuse. What is one to make of amorphous structures formulating themselves anew under different circumstances, choosing temporary leaders for a time, then being glad to let them go, acquiring only such size and permanence as immediate advantage indicates? Their principle is precisely to avoid paying the costs of a permanent structure of power.

These headless groups can be politically potent. They are numerous, small, and unencumbered. They travel light. They are difficult to defeat because there are so many of them, and they do not stay in one place (or one shape, for that matter) for too long. Beaten down here, they rise elsewhere.

No doubt these headless groups suffer distinct disabilities. They lack permanent leadership. They find it difficult to develop expertise. Committing their membership is no easy task. But they do not have to do it alone. By forming temporary coalitions with more hierarchical groups when their interests coincide, they combine their enthusiasm and adaptability with the advantages of the more settled and sustaining presence of their allies.

Coalitions allow specialization and division of labor without raising questions about who is in charge.[33] Different groups lead on different issues. The *ad hoc* arrangement permits internal differences among public interest groups as well. Hierarchical public interest groups, more interested in evidence and more willing to deal with the center, such as Common Cause and the Sierra Club, engage directly with established institutions. Sectarian public interest groups clash with the establishment or go to court to invoke generalized norms against it. Taken together, both mildly hierarchical and extreme sectarian forms of organization complement one another most successfully.

This combination of somewhat different groups (as well, of course, as the resonance they evoke in the general population) explains the success of their sustained assault on environmental and safety policy.

To summarize what is already a bare-bone summary, the long-run absence of a hereditary elite and the presence of strong market and voluntary organizations in America have historically led to an admixture of political cultures. Thus the establishment alliance of hierarchy and markets has brought about two types of conflict — a civic balance model in which an element of hierarchy seeks to strengthen government to provide countervailing power to markets, and a sectarian attack on establishment principles proper. During times of crisis — war, cold war, depression — these differences are submerged and public support for the more divisive border sectarianism is diminished. Then, in the medium-range, the vast increase in education and the growth of service industries, both of which made hierarchy less essential after the Second World War, broadened the base of support for sectarian appeals. The civil rights movement and the revolt against the Vietnam War provided models for imitation. And in the short-run, the availability of sectarian political entrepreneurs and the existence of effective technology to mobilize a mail-order membership facilitated the success of public interest groups. That is why America has become border country.

In the past, the designation "sect" has usually been modified by "powerless," as established forces suppressed it or it rejected the larger society. This is no longer so in America. A distinguishing feature of our time is that sectarian groups can use government to impose restrictive regulations on their enemies instead of the other way around. This explains the extraordinary combination of bureaucracy (enforcing regulations on opponents) without authority. For sectarians themselves, while invoking government, are not inclined to respect it. The weakening of all integrative institutions designed to mediate between the citizen and the state — political parties, trade unions, churches — on a broad basis across a spectrum of issues, and the strengthening of single-issue special interest groups, is attributable, we suggest, to the rise of sectarianism.

IX

The Dialogue is Political

They will never agree, said Sidney Smith about two Edinburgh
women hurling insults at each other from the top windows of
their tenements; they are arguing from different premises.
According to our theory of culture, center and border are
doing just that. Their views about risk are not to be considered
as independent ideas or personal preferences so much as public
statements topping different social structures. So long as their
loyalties are turned toward centers or borders, people will buy
a whole package of political judgments about nature, human
and physical, that go with center or border views. On other
issues they use their private discretion, but as rational beings
and social beings they exercise their freedom by choosing the
social institutions around them. Having chosen for the sect,
they slide their decisions onto the arguments that feed sectarian life; having chosen for the center, they slide their decisions onto center-supporting institutions. Then they are
immune to reason from the other side, since center and border
are structured by mutual opposition.

We have described three institutional types which take some
part in public decision-making, two that uphold the center,
market and hierarchy, and one representing the border, sect.
Each provides a theory of how society should be organized and

a set of smooth grooves into which a life style can be cast. Each also provides an explanatory philosophy to justify it. These three types arise out of an interest in power, either for exerting it or for checking it.[1]

It is axiomatic for the cultural approach that none of these institutional schemes with their justifying cosmologies is mysteriously imposed upon individuals from the outside. Each only endures to the extent that its subscribers see no viable alternatives. Or put the other way, each is only strong enough to attract support when it is strong enough to blind its adherents to the virtues of other ways. This means that the fundamental principles have to be constantly repolished and commitment to them expressed in judgment about small practical arrangements as well as about great matters of state. Such basic principles act as premises that separate debaters on risk, partly because they provide some intellectual coherence and mainly because they can be appealed to as arbiters in everyday life. In domestic rituals (as well as in public affairs), they provide the stuff from which letters of condolence are drawn and the source of sentiments for speeches at weddings, funerals, presentation ceremonies, and addresses of welcome and farewell. But their ritual uses are the surface functions of these basic principles. More profoundly, they serve as strings of control, credible supports for threats and promises and other techniques of moral coercion.

The first move toward understanding the debate on risk is to come down off the rooftops and examine the foundations of each set of arguments. Certain questions will reveal most quickly the rival, underlying principles. For pursuing cultural analysis the guiding thread is to keep looking for the rules into which a vision of the good life can be effectively translated and for the possibilities of praise and censure that can commit members. First we look for the good vision of human destiny that is upheld by one or the other of the quarters of the cultural spectrum. For or against the center, for or against market or hierarchy, the strongest attack rests on some positive ideal. Instead of looking at the anger and hurt that surface in

the debate, we burrow down to find the hopeful expectations
that could be realized if certain rules were kept and would be
jeopardized if they were broken. This good vision and its
promises can be used for holding people in their roles and for
blaming them if they weaken. Conversely, each form of cultural bias has its own related explanations of suffering and failure, the complementary aspect of its positive ideals.[2] And if it
is ever to be actualized in practical living, it must also give
individuals some way of dealing with their envy of each other.
When we have followed how each institutional type satisfies
these basic requirements, we will see how its very success ex-
poses it to temptations that threaten to destroy its hopes. Even
a cursory glimpse of the cultural foundations will make it
easier to see why one kind of society selects certain dangers for
attention while ignoring others produced by itself.

Needless to say, in real life ideals are never systematically
connected with practical rules of behavior. Each of the three
schemes must turn out to be incoherent. Either the principles
are self-contradictory, or when translated into rules for living
they generate mutually incompatible regulations, or inconsis-
tency shows up between the ideas and the kind of life that is
lived in their name. Fortunately people can tolerate a lot of
incoherence. Institutions effectively screen some contradictions from sight. But as new resources appear they cause redis-
tributions of wealth and power. If these are weighty enough to
challenge existing arrangements, they expose the intellectual
weaknesses of any particular scheme for living. Only personal
commitment can ensure stability. Their capability for being
rationalized gives these three forms of cultural bias some
potential to be stable, but at any time persons can switch their
allegiance by bringing the principles to ridicule. So at the basis
of the risk arguments we look for something approaching,
however precariously, a coherent view of society.

Attitudes toward social inequality are a good touchstone for
comparing the three institutional types. Social inequality is the
challenge to conscience that prizes moral principle apart from
moral practice. For a starting point we do not look for an

imaginary state of nature but take the three types at a place at which each is fully subscribing to democratic principles and the rule of law. Each has arrived at a point at which moral problems about social inequality have been satisfactorily settled. According to the genius of each type, everyone can with sincerity say that in some definable sense human beings are equal before the law. From here we can try to deduce what elaborations of principle would be necessary to sustain each of the social types.

The sectarian view does not tolerate inequality in any form: its big promise is to introduce equality all around. We showed above that equal distribution is implied in the conditions of rational, voluntary association. The practical judgment in favor of equality needs a more general philosophic justification than the mere requirements of a particular form of organization. So the sect tends publicly to express a faith in human goodness and the supreme value of the individual from which it derives its other guiding principles. (We saw in the more sectarian organizations of the environmental movement how this faith is invoked.) For a sect the challenge of living in a developing political society is to hold firmly onto the faith by which it is inspired. At least the sect has a direct way of dealing with envy. Instead of being repressed or diverted, envy can be recruited to the sect's cause as an active principle of control. It stimulates the effort of mutual criticism that keeps the society free of artificial distinctions.

In our analysis, however, this vision of a free society of equals needs to be guaranteed by more than the keen concern of its members. It also needs a stable opposing center against which to define itself as a border and it needs scope for expansion. Sectarians tend to be oblivious of these particular needs. Outsiders can see that certain risks to the way of life chosen by sectarians come from too much success in establishing it: overattachment to its boundary against the outside and too much success campaigning against the power of the center. To these inherent dangers we shall return below. The present issue is concerned only with intellectual and moral contradictions.

Being unable to expand and split (for whatever reason) leads sectarians to unedifying anger against each other. Expulsion is the readiest solution, but justifying expulsion leads to denying the essential goodness of human nature. For the sect, the ultimate contradiction is to deny the equality of humans. As the sect develops its political career, when it is faced with restriction, it finds itself dividing the race between good humans, fully entitled to civic rights, and bad ones who arguably are not. It follows that in the course of its life history, the sect engages from time to time in a debate on whose outcome hangs the integrity of its purposes. This crucial debate is about the right to use violence against oppressive government. Once arbitrary violence wins over legitimate authority, the sect has betrayed its faith.

We can also take market as a system committed to social equality as well as to the equality of citizens before the law. But market is less wholehearted from the start about social equality than is the sectarian vision of how the world should be. In a market society any citizen has the right to enter the system of exchanges that constitute the main institutions and to benefit from the immunities and protections devised to make the exchanges work. But it is bound to accept temporary inequalities, resulting from the ups and downs of the market, since it requires that success in fair competition be rewarded. Its big promise is individual success. Its fundamental justification is not faith in the value of the individual but faith in the freedom to exchange. It deals with envy obliquely by first ensuring that the rules of exchange are fair and then assuming that the social rankings that emerge are not necessarily permanent. It likes to prove this by honoring those who have progressed from rags to riches. It further stops complaints of inequality by fixing blame on the losers. The claim that humans are equal citizens is not diminished by admitting that they are not equally endowed with personal qualifications for success, so the failures feel too guilty to complain.

In our analysis, the good vision that this kind of society holds out has to be underwritten by one necessary condition. The social system needs enough turbulence for social distinctions to be blurred as soon as they are formed. If neither expanding markets nor changes in the pattern of values can produce this equalizing effect, there are other means for doing it. No Western society has ever embraced the market system so thoroughly as various peoples of Papua. Here we find that tremendous social pressures enforce redistribution of a rich man's property on his heirs.[3]

Too much confidence in the market system may weaken the censure that stops individuals from acquiring permanent advantages. Too much success in establishing market as a way of life generally blinds its adherents to the inevitability of individual failure. Long-term concentrations of wealth make it impossible to give honest answers to the challenge of envy: with wealth stabilized, the premise of equality is flouted. Where there is one law for the rich and one for the poor, faith in the value of free exchange is under challenge. Instead of individual failure being random, something that could happen in any family without loss of power to recuperate, a large and permanent underclass poses grave social problems that the prevailing philosophy cannot solve.[4] When privilege of birth becomes necessary for success in the market place, the unprivileged are found lacking the minimal resources for exercising a citizen's rights. Something near to a third of the population[5] have to be either ignored or helped with public charity—this in violation of political principles. A large number even have to be consigned to institutional care, their helplessness provoking an unconvincing casuistry around their right to vote and their civic incapacity. Here, too, some crucial internal debates tend to be engaged concerning the plausibility of the system's fundamental values: how to control monopolistic tendencies, whether to redistribute wealth, what to do about sturdy beggars. On the answers to these questions the market type of society holds to its vision or loses it.

Hierarchy does not teach that social equality is necessary, good, or possible. It never aims to establish it. Inequality is written into its constitution. The big promises it holds out to its followers are stability and dignity, thanks to an encompassing doctrine of the hallowed relation of a whole to its parts. This is the fundamental value. Hierarchy can produce some elegantly complex metaphysics for integrating individual freedom before the law with inequality for the sake of the whole organism. Its institutions deal with envy by insulating compartments, separating life styles, and setting ceilings on aspirations. Its special vision of man in society has to be protected by controlling information and by channeling wealth to established authority. Contrary to the market system that loses moral plausibility if the pattern of wealth holding is stabilized, hierarchy needs to stabilize control of wealth. Since new resources upset the pattern of distribution, hierarchy is usually intent on slowing down the rate of change.

Hierarchy relies on explicit controls, whereas market relies on indirect controls and sectarians repudiate controls, relying on goodness of heart. Here again, the hierarchical society is especially vulnerable when it is too successful. Strong censorship leads to loss of information from a changing world beyond its control and to constraints on individual initiative. So hierarchy becomes a tempting prey to external enemies. Of this it tends to be well aware and its interest in risk is much concerned with foreign politics. So long as information is tightly controlled, there is not much worrisome contradiction among the founding principles or incompatibility between them and the way of life they justify. It is difficult to break out of such a system intellectually. Censorship works well when it is self-imposed or even voluntarily accepted by a population content with what it knows or fearful of new knowledge. But if it has to be enforced coercively, censorship ends the civil guarantees, destroys dignity, and shifts the polity to tyranny of the privileged part over the rest, thus violating faith in a benign part/whole relationship.

This much delving into the cultural foundations opens the possibility of seeing what polite dialogue about risk would be like. Since the abusive remarks are only surface manifestations of disagreement, real dialogue means adapting the institutions nearer to one another's ideal. And this happens all the time. The dialogue is always on. Market and sect being less stable than hierarchy, both often find the unconsidered effects of their system lead them to adopt hierarchical principles. Suppose that the promises of sect and market have been subverted and now, instead of a conversation between different views, the political life of the whole society is conducted according to hierarchical principles. With closure on information all around, the main risks will have to do with war: hostility between separate sovereign states or civil war. If the risk is perceived, the sensible way to manage the conversation will be for the hierarchists to create roles for market individualists with promise of private gain. For the individualists never like to see the debate closed, they hate to draw fixed boundaries, and their obvious interest is in free movement of persons and resources and in profitable alliances. Market and hierarchy make a formidably stable combination.

But in this new dialogue, in which the voice of sectarianism has temporarily been submerged, suppose market were to win hierarchy away from its self-defeating love of secrecy and censorship, mocking and making its adherents ashamed of their wish to keep knowledge under social control. Then market could easily become the dominant voice. What risks would the people encounter then? Being poor in a rich society is not easy to bear. And the race to riches may leave the countryside barren. Market individualists need to call hierarchy back into the conversation to protect the weak and to keep an eye on the long-term resource base. But how is the individualist ever going to see the need for hierarchy? Never, unless the voice from the border, shocked at injustice and waste, creates a public scandal. Then the market is forced to compromise with hierarchy and the two occupy the center once more and the sectarians are pushed into the border.

Once or twice in Western history sectarians have emerged from the border as a powerful force, briefly dominating the political debate in the turmoil before and after great wars. Once they take to arms or accede to power, they transform themselves into little hierarchies, very strict in censorship and restrictive about civic rights. Suppose they could dominate the political scene and still keep their guiding vision; then the whole center would be weakened by sectarian attack. In this event, it is credible that the environment would be protected, less credible that there would be less risk of aggressive war. There would inevitably be neglect of the technical and institutional apparatus of political life, since sectarianism is set against technology and institutions. The Dutch dikes against the sea would never have been built, nor would nuclear power reactors be safely maintained. The biggest and most immediate risk, however, would be to the civic rights of the individual, not merely the risk of being born a second-class citizen in a hierarchy or of becoming one of the human derelicts which litter the market place but the risk of being classified as evil, a malefactor outside the protection of the law.

The sectarian border is a kind of permanent opposition that has no intention of governing, disapproves of government, and develops no capacity for exercising power. From this follow its real, practical difficulties of keeping in the debate. Since sectarian activities weaken the political center and restrict the economic room in society, the border is liable to weaken its two conditions of support. When the center cannot be counted upon, and the ordinary activities of government cannot be taken for granted, all hell breaks loose. Common Cause, perhaps the most important public interest organization devoted to improving government, tries to bring countervailing power to bear when the center is too strong for the citizen's good. At first it insists upon open meetings and freedom of information. But once the center weakens, Common Cause sees the guarantees of liberty, which its civic balance program was devised to perfect, being called into question. At this point it begins to shore up the political parties, realizing that if the center exerts no pull, the push from the periphery can knock it all down.[6]

In addition to needing a center, sects and other border units need to split and expand. Schism is part of their constitution. Because they cannot handle internal tension and because they have no way to settle disputes except by expulsion, sectarians need plenty of room. The ability of the United States to dispense with a strong hierarchical center with differentiated status has been attributed to room for geographical expansion. Able to split off and make a new life when internal pressures mounted, the original sectarian groups used to find a safety valve in the frontier. The recent equivalent of a physical frontier has been an expanding economy. As wealth increased, various groups were able to insulate themselves from one another without raising the fateful question of whether more for one necessarily meant less for another. Yet a shrinking economy and an expanding bureaucracy cannot avoid this confrontation.

The worst outlook for sectarian principles follows when, facing the declining tax base of an economy set to no growth, government tries to rationalize its activities. Programs must become more uniform. More regulations allow fewer exceptions. Deviance becomes less tolerable. Sectarian leaders find they are not allowed to enjoy government subsidy while evading control. They are tempted then to become part of the despised central system, joining the hierarchies, submitting evidence, and accepting judgments according to the accepted center procedures. Doing so they may be rejected by their own membership. Their new dilemma is how to escape from bureaucracy while building it up. They worry about technological risk, but risk reduction requires rules. Government is forced to grow more intrusive. Bureaucracy increases. The costs of risk prevention grow; so does the size of the organizations, causing private industry to be organized in larger units in order to afford the price. It will be evident that the accusation that large organizations are getting larger is justified. So sectarianism creates consequences that reaffirm its view of the world.

The unintended results of a full flowering of sectarian politics would be a larger, weaker government and a smaller economy. The economy would shrink as resources are used to prevent dangers; the bureaucracy would grow as it regulates the risks people are allowed to take. There will be many more rules, true; but since the rulers will not be respected, their authority to regulate will also be undermined. Government will be bigger, but it will not be stronger; openness and participation will only lead to unanswerable criticism. For the society in general this will mean enhanced conflict over the distribution of a smaller pie, without a cohesive center to moderate the resulting disputes. Nor will a larger public sector and a smaller private sector be good for sectarian groups, for they especially depend on a tolerant larger society.

The sectarian prophecies that power corrupts and that larger institutions corrupt more absolutely come true as shackled government strives to perform the regulatory tasks they lay upon it. Their prophecy that the world outside will not prosper comes true as they demand restrictions on economic growth. While berating the inhumane, mechanical operation of bureaucracy, they work to bring it about. When the private as well as the public sectors have less scope for variety, sectarianism is going to be suppressed by popular edict. So sectarianism unbridled leads to its own self-fulfilling, self-defeating end. Sectarians have every reason to worry about the dismal future. No more than it would be good for hierarchists or market individualists, it would not be good for sectarians to have their own views dominate the political conversation. For the sake of that conversation, it is best to recognize that sectarians can never be satisfied. If intensive effort were devoted to reducing risk, sectarians would not feel they had won what they wanted, and there would be no hope that they would then support the political system that favored them. To the innocent-sounding question, "How much safety is enough?" their answer is that there can never be enough.

Risk, like worldliness, is an ideal target for criticism. It is immeasurable and its unacceptability is unlimited. The closer the community moves toward sharing their views, the faster the sectarian groups move on to new demands. Their political organization depends on making steep demands on the outside world. There can never be sufficient holiness or safety.

Suppose life expectancy were expressly allocated by government: how much should be spent on all lives together? No doubt a huge amount. But since other purposes must also be served by government, there would be a form of resource allocation. But if the question were rephrased to ask how much should be spent on you or me, the only answer could be "everything," for to ourselves and our loved ones we are irreplaceable and priceless. As beings of infinite worth we would require every precaution. Separated from any consideration of alternative uses for resources (that is, separated from considering our fellow human beings), each of us is likely to demand much more of government than we could were we the government that decided for all. Since the sources of risk are virtually infinite in number, subject only to the fertility of the imagination, there is no limit on what can be spent on eliminating them.

This harsh judgment on extreme sectarian policy only matches the notorious judgments against market competitiveness and bureaucratic stagnation. Seen in their worst light, all three forms of cultural bias are contradictory and self-defeating. Each sees particular dangers and fails to see others of its own producing. When the argument about risks of technology is locked in stalemate, it is good to know the assumptions on which each debating position is grounded. A second marriage, Dr. Johnson said, reveals the triumph of hope over experience. At the heart of efforts to further the dialogue between border and center lies a contradiction between the desire for debate and the realization that discussion has proven unproductive. It is easy enough to say let there be dialogue, for a pluralistic society should work out the accommodation between initially rival and hostile views. But our analysis shows why the rival perspectives are polarized, each selecting facts to support pre-existing perceptions of risk. At least we know better now than to wish to see the erosion of the center or the suppression of the border.

Conclusion:

Risk is a Collective Construct

The aim of this book has been to understand the social forces
that speak on behalf of environmental protection in America.
The movement that now defends the natural environment
from the effects of technology is allied to similar movements in
Europe. All have emerged in the last twenty years, though they
are different in each country. Here is a case of cultural change
to which cultural analysis can be applied. The argument
pursued here is not easy however. The idea that public perception of risk and its acceptable levels are collective constructs, a
bit like language and a bit like aesthetic judgment, is hard to
take. The central thesis that the selection of dangers and the
choice of social organization run hand in hand goes against the
grain of contemporary thought. It could need to be substanti-
ated with an account of the conditions of knowledge, which is
beyond our capacity, or at least with an account of reality,
especially the reality of physical dangers, which is beyond our
scope.

That perceptions of right and truth depend on cultural categories created along with the social relations they are used for
defending has been recognized by a philosophical tradition
since the nineteenth century. The more we draw on this tradition, the more we are beset with charges of relativism. These

we can try to meet in various ways. One way (as in the previous chapter) is to describe with impartial care the deducible consequences of preferring one form of social organization over others. There is nothing relativistic in this exercise. It is performed by standing firmly in one critical perspective and saying what can be seen from there. Another way is to expose some inconsistencies in current thinking about risk (as we did in chapters III and IV). The strongest defense is to make as persuasive as possible the case for three different views about risk emanating from three types of social organization. To develop the typology, some blunt instruments from anthropology and political theory have been useful for shaking ethnocentric parochialism.

The first issue in any argument about risk is to agree on which risks are most worrisome. The choice to worry most about risks of human violence (war, terrorism, or crime), risks from technology, or risks from economic failure is basic. We submit that the choice is never made directly but is settled by a preference among kinds of favored social institutions. If it is true, as psychological tests suggest, that the private person does not pay attention to remote probabilities, that finding has to be qualified. Our cultural theory shows that the most relevant of improbable bad outcomes have been anticipated by the private person in a prior social commitment. The least downturn of the stock market makes the market individualist break out in a sweat, long before it seems to anyone else to threaten the stability of future market operations. The least threat to law and order or news of foreign weaponry sets the hierarchist in a tremble, long before it seems likely to others that rioting or invasion is imminent. Similarly, the more sectarian branches of the environmental movement takes seriously a small deterioration in the quality of the air, for fear of what more distant risks it may portend. These cares for long-term remote probabilities of disaster (being carried in institutions) are habitually excluded in the psychologists' experiments by the form of the questions and the selection of subjects. But they could start again by framing their questions and designing their research so as to invest their matter with more social significance. Analysis of this kind[1] recognizes different types of cultures resulting from their members' sustained attention to feasible social goals. Three have seemed sufficient for the thesis being argued. Two of these derive from the established stock of political thought in the West, market individualism and hierarchy. Neither encompasses the structure and goals of the environmental movement. For this purpose we needed to develop a third model of rational behavior under institutional constraints, the type we have called sectarian. Each of the three types are necessarily given in extreme forms. Most enduring polities establish some exchange of ideas between them and reach a temporary compromise. Cultural bias only becomes apparent when the argument has tipped conspicuously to one side or another. We have identified the starting point of the questions about acceptable risk. The answer is that the risks of war are not acceptable to the hierarchist because he is focused on dangers of foreign relations, but his intelligence is so bad he often is an unreliable authority on the subject of whether the risks are real or not. Risks of economic collapse are ever present to the mind of the market individualist, but he cannot be relied upon to know how to prevent it. Risks from technology are uppermost in the sectarian mind, but that does not guarantee accurate prediction any more than in the other two cases. This is where the charge of relativism hurts our case. The questions of our first chapter can be returned to us. If every position is sustained by a social commitment, how can our effort to examine social commitments take us any further? How can we know whether the dangers are actually increasing or whether we are more afraid? How can we discount our own commitment? The center takes one view of risk, the border takes another. Is there any judgment possible between their views?

Any form of life can be justified. Among kings and republics, voting systems, kinds of family life and child-rearing, no one is to say that one is better or worse. How can there be any judging between life styles and moral ends? This problem usually stops any attempt to compare ethical systems and it would seem to block taking further any argument about perception of risks. Some, however, would exempt the border from the general criticism; when the center starts to talk, it is betrayed by the ballast of social commitment carried with its particular view; it is indeed the essence of the border claim that center views are embedded in social strategies. The border claims to have more credibility, itself being freer from entangling social purposes. But we have also shown that the border is not immune. Border theories emanate from its social predicament of chosen voluntariness. In the process of solving the formidable problems of voluntary organization, it forms and declares its views about danger and conspiracy. So it is not one whit more independent than are hierarchists and individualists.

There are some similar, well-known arguments in favor of border claims. Power corrupts, the border shuns power: this gives it the rights of innocence, even of disinterestedness. In further support of border claims a sturdy tradition holds that the truest insights come with distance. According to this tradition, the outsider sees more clearly and renewal comes from the margins of society: if the center were to ignore the sayings of shaggy prophets, it would close itself to criticism and lose the power of reform. On this theory, deeply entrenched, the center is too constricted in its casing of institutional habits: no change ever comes from the center, all innovation comes from without, and sometimes, so obdurate is the center, it must come violently. But since this theory of exogenous change merely reiterates border values, it brings them no independent support. The center does not usually accept that centers are incapable of internal reform. To claim that the border speaks from a privileged standpoint is special border pleading. The center makes the parallel claim to a privileged view because of the responsibilities it carries. Our problem from the outset has been to assess their opposing claims. One remaining course is to try to identify the kind of society that an ethical theory is being used to build; perhaps we can choose which we would prefer to live in.

All three positions, individualism, hierarchy, and sectarianism, are extremes. None is prima facie attractive. The ruthlessness of power seeking in a free market society has been exposed often enough in literature and in history and even in children's stories. The clogged inertia and cruel caste distinctions of hierarchy similarly are a butt of satire. No one would choose to live in either type of society unless he were strong enough to compete successfully in the first or privileged by birth in the second. In spite of the notorious defects, both have their defenders too, so there is no need to rehearse further their respective merits and failures.

By comparison, though the merits of the sectarian way of life are praised by its champions, its defects are hidden. By way of evening the score, we here list the main failings that can be deduced from its social situation. The border tends to present humans as victims to be compensated and weaklings to be protected. So long as the border refuses to take power and so long as there is a center to blame, by apportioning blame to power the border maintains the distribution of power that justifies its philosophy. If the worst risks are incurred involuntarily, we are all helpless victims of a fate we cannot escape and if risk taking unleashes irreversible destruction, humanity has no options in the future. Pessimism underlies the sectarian view more deeply than its surface optimism about the essential goodness of human nature. To believe that human involvement in social life has been one long, unwished for, exploitative deception denies any redeeming promise in the social order. Starting from such disgust and despair, it plausibly fixes attention on self-destructive features of modern life. If the exploiters were an identifiable, punishable class, revolution would be the program and the whole social process would not be indicted in its essence. But the implicit charge is that all mankind is victimized by its own inherently evil nature. Paradoxically, when being asked to join the saving movement, humans are said to hold their destiny in their own hands, but the saving doctrine assumes them collectively to be beings inadequate for the task. This secular version of original sin is more gloomy than Augustine's or Luther's, for there is no gleam of hope from outside, no faith in divine intervention.

By contrast, the center is more hopeful. The border is entitled to challenge its optimism. Why more hopeful? Not on logical reasoning or from experience but from similar gut convictions with which there is no arguing. Starting with the individualists, their market institutions do not draw them to dwell on fundamental principles at all, still less on what has gone wrong with world history. Individualism is optimistic by default, its principles being largely pragmatic. For its part, hierarchy can only survive by the strength of a commitment to structure and meaning in the universe. Its optimism, like the pessimism of sectarians, inheres in its institutional life.

Seen from the center, the border view of human society appears inconsistent because it is a call to action in the name of humanity resting on a theory of human inadequacy for social organization. The emphasis on individuality and equality seems to put human capability for social intercourse into the background. Nature, only sparsely occupied by people, fills the foreground. To buy a border view of the risks that threaten the world, centrist judgments would have to be revised as to the value of civilization and urban life and as to the capacity of humans to bear the tensions and distress of living together. There is no reasoning with tastes and preferences. Assumptions about freedom and responsibility either follow from or lead to the choice between social forms—it makes no difference which way the process works. In the end, we either favor a centrist view of the human predicament, or we favor the sectarian view, or we prefer not to choose.

After this recognition of subjective starting points we hardly need to negotiate the hurdles of philosophical relativism. According to this critical approach, our so-called method of cultural analysis would be no more than the illegitimate elevation of one perspective to the status of a theory. At least we have gone to pains to show three perspectives from within the standpoint of commonly accepted social theory. If it were a scientific theory, the relativist critique continues, it could be tried out and tested operationally. But a social theory is so political that it is bound to work only if it appeals to enough people because they will decide to apply it. A political prophecy fulfills itself by majority rule. It will appeal if it is framed in the context of shared convictions. If a million readers say, "Aha! Now I understand what I did not understand before," it is nothing. Relativism says that a million in agreement after reading the argument are no more than the million who agreed before. The argument may articulate a favorite view but converts no one. Of course, this argument that demotes the sectarian view from its place of privilege will be understood because a lot of people understand the general problem already.

This kind of relativist criticism lacks a theory of how a so-called cognitive scheme ever gets its initial boundaries. It supposes there is no taking in of new ideas; one can only rearrange a new experience so that it conforms to what one knows already. It supposes that translation imposes our categories of thought upon a foreign author, leaving our own cognitive *status quo* unchanged. If they are seriously to argue counter to the history of intellectual change, relativist critics need a theory of the nontransmissibility of ideas. They imply that each thinker is a prisoner inside his definable cognitive scheme, but how he got there and how its boundaries got fixed must surely depend on cultural theory. Cultural analysis rejects the model of the cognitive prison because so long as social change is possible, values and perceptions can change too. The risk debate itself is a record of rapid cultural change. If there is such a thing as a cognitive scheme, it is not carved in granite.

Instead of the old recurrent imagery of knowledge as a solid thing, bounded or mapped out, we prefer the idea of knowledge as the changing product of social activity. It is not so much like a building, eventually to be finished, but more like an airport, always under construction. It has been compared to an open-ended communal enterprise, to a ship voyaging to an unknown destination but never arriving and never dropping anchor. It is like a many-sided conversation in which being ultimately right or wrong is not at issue. What matters is that the conversation continue with new definitions and solutions and terms made deep enough to hold the meanings being tried. Cultural analysis would be undermining its own conditions for producing conviction if it were teaching that every social situation generates its own truth and that there are as many truths as there are communities. That path is not toward intellectual liberation. Cultural analysis need not become a conversation stopper which allows anyone to block an argument by referring reductively to its social genesis. Its own claims to attention would be destroyed at the same stroke. This provides a procedure for inquiry that can accommodate the social context of belief without cutting out the basis of discourse.

We cannot conclude without reverting to the subject of risk itself. The social sciences are responsible for part of the confusion about risk. The wrong division between the reality of the external world and the gropings of the human psyche have allocated real knowledge to the physical sciences and illusions and mistakes to the field of psychology. Causality in the external world is generally treated as radically distinct from the results of individual perception. According to this approach, risk is a straightforward consequence of the dangers inherent in the physical situation, while attitudes toward risk depend on individual personalities. When particular risks are objectively ascertainable, it follows that the gap between the expert and the lay public ought to be closed in only one direction—toward the opinion of experts: the lay public must be taught the facts; the scientific message must be clearly labeled. When experts disagree, this can also be attributed to inadequate understanding or to human weakness; even an expert may sell out, whether to industry, if he is speaking on one side of the debate, or to an antibusiness ideology, if speaking on the other. On this telling, a chasm separates perception (which goes on inside the psyche) from the physical facts (which exist outside).

When psychologists concentrate on subjective perception

and find that high levels of risk are barely perceived by some people while horrifying to others, their explanation looks for universal psychic laws of cognition or for personality traits. A subjectivist approach also assumes that individuals have attitudes toward risk in general rather than some attitudes toward certain kinds of risks and different attitudes toward others. The whole personality, confronting risk as a whole, is expected to be biased either toward risk taking or toward risk avoiding. Working with such assumptions, psychologists do not try to explain why some people fear environmental more than other kinds of dangers.

The main questions posed by the current controversies over risk show the inappropriateness of dividing the problem betwen objectively calculated physical risks and subjectively biased individual perceptions. The sudden appearance of intense public concern about the environment can never be explained by evidence of harm from technology. Weighing the balance between harm and help is not a purely technical question. Technology is a source of help as well as harm. Objective evidence about technology in general is not going to take us very far. Acceptable risk is a matter of judgment and nowadays judgments differ. Between private, subjective perception and public, physical science there lies culture, a middle area of shared beliefs and values. The present division of the subject that ignores culture is arbitrary and self-defeating.

Standing inside our own culture, we can only look at our predicament through our culturally fabricated lens. The apparatus of scientific investigation is as unique to our civilization as are its results. The conceptual tools of economic analysis are entirely our own invention. The specialized techniques of risk assessment have never been tried by any civilization before us. Our survey methods for testing public opinion and laboratory methods for studying human reasoning powers are unique, too. However proud we are of advances in the physical sciences, everyone admits that the social sciences are not at the same high peak. And then there is the problem that physical science is moving all the time. So there is scope for reasonable disagreement. Any accepted method of inquiry imposes control upon curiosity. At any one time there are questions which cannot be formulated, still less asked or answered. But in each generation something can be asked that could not be asked before. Ours has a special experience of other cultures and expertise in assessing cultural bias. New kinds of questions bring new procedures for finding answers.[2] We have learned enough about cultural bias to recognize moral and political issues underlying a debate about physical risks. The way to end the stalemate of ethical relativism is to bring our moral and political judgment to bear openly on the basic assumptions. This is what we have tried to do.

Finally, it is fair to expect that our book has some positive conclusions about risk management. If we cannot know the risks we face, how can we cope with unknown dangers? Taking the focus of the debate away from risks and safety to the choice between social institutions, we can suggest the qualities necessary for dealing with risks.

Relative safety is not a static but rather a dynamic product of learning from error over time. Pioneers always pay the costs of premature development. First models are rarely reliable; as experience accumulates, bugs are eliminated and incompatibilities alleviated. The fewer the trials and the fewer mistakes to learn from, the more error remains uncorrected. As development continues into the second and succeeding generations, the costs of error detection and correction are shared to some extent with future practitioners and the benefits passed back down to the originators. Therefore we look for the most efficient and flexible ways of dealing with the unexpected. Risk aversion is a preoccupation with anticipating danger that leads to large-scale organization and centralization of power in order to mobilize massive resources against possible evils. The probability that any known danger will occur declines because of anticipatory measures. But the probability that if the unexpected happens it will prove catastrophic increases, because resources required for response have been used up in anticipation.

There are also more subtle ways in which attempted control, by creating a false sense of security, compromises coping ability. The dependence of Bay Area Rapid Transit on a computerized scheduling system that would make no errors, for example, led to a disregard for coping with breakdowns that were never supposed to occur. "The classic example here is the *Titanic,* where the new ability to control most kinds of leaks led to the understocking of lifeboats, the abandonment of safety drills and disregard of reasonable caution in navigation."[3]

It should be of interest to the environmental movement to know that evidence from ecological management suggests that anticipation to secure stability is a bad bet for safety. Without continuous experience in overcoming a variety of disturbances, organisms are likely to adapt to a steady state. When dramatic change does occur, these organisms are more likely to perish both because the search for stability has used up surplus resources and because they have suppressed their capacity to cope with the unexpected. The ability to learn from errors and to gain experience in coping with a wide variety of difficulties, has proved a greater aid to preservation of the species than efforts to create a narrow band of controlled conditions within which they would flourish for a time but which leaves trees, crops, and animals vulnerable to more severe damage when things change. Resilience is the capacity to use change to better cope with the unknown; it is learning to bounce back.

Ecologist C. S. Holling compares control by anticipation and the capacity to cope resiliently:

Resilience determines the persistence of relationships within a system. . . .

Stability on the other hand [which we call anticipation], is the ability of a system to return to an equilibrium state after a temporary disturbance. . . .

With these definitions in mind a system can be very resilient and still fluctuate greatly, i.e. have low stability. I have touched above on examples like the spruce budworm forest community in which the very fact of low stability seems to introduce high resilience. Nor are such cases isolated ones, as Watt has shown in his analysis of thirty years of data collected for every major forest insect throughout Canada by the Insect Survey program of the Canada Department of the Environment.[4]

From the standpoint of managing risk, the dilemma is posed by the polar opposites of anticipation and resilience. Anticipation emphasizes uniformity; resilience stresses variability. Applied in the current energy context, resilience would rely on variety. Instead of attempting to guard against every evil, only the most likely or most dangerous would be covered, with the full expectation that whatever was missed would be countered as and after it occurred. The implication for energy policy would be to avoid relying exclusively on any single source or mode of generation so that, whatever happened to supplies or technology, we would be able to respond resiliently. Solar energy, with its small size and independence of central coordination, is highly desirable to develop; it is less likely to be knocked out all at once with one blow. It would prove vulnerable to climatic change or an unforeseen demand for continuous high bursts of energy, dangers against which nuclear power is safer. When the one sure thing is that we won't be able to predict important difficulties that the nation will face in the future, diversity and flexibility may be the best defenses. Attempting to reduce risk by extinguishing variety may actually increase it.

If some degree of risk is inevitable, suppressing it in one place often merely moves it to another. Shifting risks may be more dangerous than tolerating them, both because those who face new risks may be unaccustomed to them and because those who no longer face old ones may become more vulnerable when conditions change.

The more we trust future generations to choose wisely (or, at least, no worse than we would), the less we need to pass specific forms of physical life on to them. Obviously, if we care about our progeny, we want to leave them better off. Obviously also, it matters who is to judge what is good for the future—they or we. By leaving them with generalized resources — knowledge, craft skills, institutions in good working order, mutual trust — the people of the future will have more discretionary power. If the selection of risk is a matter of social organization, the management of risk is an organizational problem. Since we do not know what risks we incur, our responsibility is to create resilience in our institutions. But by choosing resilience, which depends on some degree of trust in institutions, we betray our bias toward the center.

Notes

Introduction: Can We Know the Risks We Face?

1. In a comprehensive analysis of 57 governmental programs designed to save lives, John D. Graham and James W. Vaupel "reveal striking disparities . . . in cost/life saved . . ." from $3,600 for mandatory passive belts in automobiles to $7,500,000 for vinyl chloride standards to $169,200,000 for a proposed rule on acrylonitrite. ("Value of a Life: What Difference Does It Make?" *Risk Analyses,* 1, 1 [March 1981], 89, 91-93.)

2. Louis Harris and Associates, *Risk in a Complex Society* (New York: Marsh and McLennan Companies, 1980). The samples were made up of 1,488 members of the public 18 years of age and older, 402 top executives from the nation's 1,506 largest companies, and 47 members of federal regulatory agencies.

3. Jerome R. Ravetz, "Public Perceptions of Acceptable Risks as Evidence for Their Cognitive, Technical, and Social Structure," in *Technological Risk: Its Perception and Handling in the European Community,* ed. Meinolf Dierkes, Sam Edwards, Rob Coppock (Cambridge, Mass.: Oelgeschlager, Gunn & Hain; and Konigstein/ Ts: Verlag Anton Hain, 1980), pp. 46-47.

4. Ibid., p. 47.

5. Baruch Fischhoff, Sarah Lichtenstein, and Paul Slovic, "Approaches to Acceptable Risk: A Critical Guide" (Prepared for Oak Ridge National Laboratory and U.S. Nuclear Regulatory Commission, 1980), pp. ii-iii.

6. Dorothy Nelkin and Michael Pollak, "Public Participation in Technological Decisions: Reality or Grand Illusion?" *Technology Review* (August/September, 1979), pp. 55-64.

7. Mary Douglas, "Cultural Bias" (Occasional Paper No. 35, Royal Anthropological Institute of Great Britain and Ireland, London: 1978).

8. Lester Lave, "Health, Safety, and Environmental Regulations," in *Setting National Priorities: Agenda for the 1980s,* ed. Joseph A. Pechman (Washington, D.C.: The Brookings Institution, 1980), pp. 134-135.

9. Robert Cameron Mitchell, "National Environmental Lobbies and the Apparent Illogic of Collective Action," in *Collective Decision Making: Applications from Public Choice Theory,* ed. Clifford S. Russell (Baltimore and London: The Johns Hopkins University Press, 1979).

10. Abraham H. Maslow, *Motivation and Personality* (New York: Harper, 1954).

11. Ronald Inglehart, *The Silent Revolution: Changing Values and Political Styles Among Western Publics* (Princeton: Princeton University Press, 1977).

12. Ibid.

I. Risks are Hidden

1. Chauncey Starr, "Social Benefit Versus Technological Risk: What is our Society Willing to Pay for Safety?" *Science,* 165 (September 19, 1969), 1232-1238.

2. Ibid.

3. Ibid.

4. Jon Elster, "Risk, Uncertainty, and Nuclear Power," *Social Science Information,* 18, 3 (London and Beverly Hills: Sage, 1979), 371-400.

5. Ibid.

6. Ibid.

7. Ibid.

8. Noel Greis, manuscript in circulation, no title or date.

9. Dagfinn Follesdal, "Some Ethical Aspects of Recombinant DNA Research," *Social Science Information,* 18, 3 (1979), 401-419.

10. Ibid.

11. Daniel Defoe, *Robinson Crusoe and the Farther Adventures* (London and Glasgow: Collins, 1953), p. 163.

II. Risks are Selected

1. Daniel Bell, "The Return of the Sacred," in *The Winding Passage: Essays and Sociological Journeys 1960-1980* (Cambridge, Mass.: ABT Associates, Inc., 1980), chap. 17, p. 332.

2. Lucien Levy-Bruhl, *La Mentalite Primitive* (Paris: F. Alcan, 1922).

3. Peter Munch, "Causes of the Medical Malpractice Insurance Crisis: Risks and Regulations," in *The Economics of Medical Malpractice,* ed. S. Rottenberg (Washington, D.C.: American Enterprise Institute, 1978).

4. R. A. Epstein, "Medical Malpractice: Its Cause and Cure," in ibid., p. 247.

5. Ibid., p. 250.

6. Ibid., pp. 252-253.

7. N. T. Greenspan, "Descriptive Analysis of Medical Malpractice Insurance Premiums, 1974-1977," *Health Care Financing Review,* 1, 2 (Fall 1979), 65-71.

8. A. L. Kroeber, *Handbook of the Indians of California,* Bulletin 78 (Washington, D.C.: Smithsonian Bureau of American Ethnology, 1925).

9. Emile Durkheim, *The Elementary Forms of the Religious Life* (London: Allen & Unwin, 1912); Franz Steiner, *Taboo* (London: Cohen and West, 1956); Mary Douglas, *Purity and Danger: An Analysis of Concepts of Pollution and Taboo* (London: Routledge & Kegan Paul, 1966).

10. E. E. Evans-Pritchard, *Witchcraft Oracles and Magic Among the Azande* (Oxford: The Clarendon Press, 1937).

11. J. D. Krige, and E. Krige, *The Realm of the Rain Queen* (London/New York: Oxford University Press, 1943).

12. Yitzchak Elam, *The Social and Sexual Roles of Hima Women: A Study of Nomadic Cattle Breeders in Nyabushozi County, Ankole, Uganda* (Manchester University Press, 1973).

13. Ibid., p. 151.

14. Louis Harris Associates, *Harris Perspective 1979: A Survey of the Public and Environmental Activists on Environment,* Report No. 59 (New York, Washington, London: 1979).

III. Scientists Disagree

1. Dick Kirschten, "The Not-So-Clean Battle Over Cleaning the Nation's Drinking Water," *National Journal,* no. 41 (October 14, 1978), pp. 1636-1640.

2. Ibid.

3. Ibid.

4. Ibid. See Richard Doll and Richard Peto, "The Causes of Cancer: Quantitative Estimates of Avoidable Risks of Cancer in the United States Today," Journal of the National Cancer Institute, 66, 6 (June 1981), 1191-1308, 1211-1285.

5. Kirschten, "The Not-So-Clean Battle," p. 1640.

6. Douglas M. Costle, "Regulatory Reform at Last?" *Town Hall Journal* (November 13, 1979), p. 402.

7. Baruch Fischhoff, Paul Slovic, and Sarah Lichtenstein, "Which Risks are Acceptable?" *Environment,* 21 (May 1979), 17-38.

8. Among the many disagreements is one over the suitability of short-term tests, such as the Salmonella mutagenesis assay (the "Ames Test"), which correlates about 90 percent with animal bio-assays. These could be used for an initial setting of priorities, but there is no settled opinion on the subject yet.

9. "OSHA Action Plan on Cancer," *Wall Street Journal* (October 11, 1978), p. 26.

10. Thomas H. Maugh II, "How Safe Is 'Safe'," *Science,* 22 (October 6, 1978), 39.

11. Samuel S. Epstein, "Cancer, Inflation, and the Failure to Regulate," *Technology Review,* 82, 3 (December/January 1980), 42-53.

12. Gio Batta Gori, "The Regulation of Carcinogenic Hazards," *Science,* 208, 4441 (April 18, 1980), 256-261. Doll and Peto support this stand (p. 1211).

13. Philip Handler, "Some Comments on Risk Assessment," in *National Research Council Current Issues and Studies,* Annual Report (Washington, D.C.: National Academy of Sciences, 1979).

14. Ibid.

15. Ibid.

16. John Higginson, "Cancer and Environment: Higginson Speaks Out," *Science,* 205, 4413 (September 28, 1979), 1363-1366.

17. Ibid.

18. Ibid.

19. Ibid.

20. Ibid.

21. Samuel S. Epstein, *The Politics of Cancer* (San Francisco: Sierra Club Books, 1978; and Garden City, New York: Anchor Press, rev. ed., 1979).

22. Richard Peto, "Distorting the Epidemiology of Cancer: The Need for a More Balanced Overview," *Nature,* 284, 5754 (March 27, 1980), 297-300.

23. Samuel S. Epstein, Letter to the Editor, *Nature,* 289, 5794 (January 15, 1981), 115-116.

24. Samuel S. Epstein and Joel B. Swartz, "Fallacies of Lifestyle Cancer Theories," *Nature,* 289, 5794 (January 15, 1981), 127-130.

25. Ibid.

26. Jane E. Brody, "Three Mile Island: No Health Impact Found," *New York Times* (April 15, 1980), pp. C1-2.

27. William W. Kellogg and Margaret Mead, ed., *The Atmosphere: Endangered and Endangering* (DHEW Publication no. NIH 77-1065), Fogarty International Center Proceedings #39. Proceedings of a conference held October 26-29, 1975 at the National Institute of Environmental Sciences, North Carolina and sponsored by the Institute and the Fogarty International Center.

28. Ibid., preface by Margaret Mead, p. xxi.

29. Ibid.

30. Ibid., p. xxiii.

31. William W. Kellogg, "The Atmosphere and Society," in ibid., p. 96.

32. James E. Lovelock, "The Interaction of the Atmosphere and the Biosphere," in ibid., p. 119.

33. Dorothy Nelkin, "Scientists in an Adversary Culture: The 1970s Program in Science, Technology and Society," paper presented to Organization of American Historians, April, 1978.

34. John Herbers, "Atomic Issue Shifts to Political Arena," *New York Times* (July 5, 1979), pp. A1, A14.

35. Handler, "Some Comments on Risk Assessment."

36. Ibid.

IV. Assessment is Biased

1. A splendid survey is Baruch Fischhoff, Paul Slovic, and Sarah Lichtenstein, "Weighing the Risks," *Environment,* 21, 4 (May 1959), 17-34.

2. See Aaron Wildavsky, "The Political Economy of Efficiency: Cost-Benefit Analysis and Program Budgeting," *Public Administration Review,* XXVI, 4 (December 1966), 292-310.

3. Howard Kunreuther, *Disaster Insurance Protection: Public Policy Lessons* (New York: Wiley, 1978).

4. Herbert A. Simon, "A Behavioral Model of Rational Choice," *Quarterly Journal of Economics,* 99 (1955), 99-118.

5. Ibid., p. 101.

6. Daniel Kahneman and Amos Tversky, "Prospect Theory: An Analysis of Decision under Risk," *Econometrica,* 47, 2 (March 1979), 263-291.

7. Aaron Wildavsky, *The Politics of the Budgetary Process,* 3d ed. (Boston: Little, Brown & Co., 1979). See also C. E. Lindblom, *The Policy Making Process* (Englewood Cliffs: Prentice-Hall, Inc., 1968).

V. The Center is Complacent

1. Paul Slovic, Baruch Fischhoff, and Sarah Lichtenstein, "Informing People About Risk," in *Banbury Report 6: Product Labeling and Health Risks,* ed. Louis A. Morris, Michael B. Mazis, Ivan Barofsky (Cold Spring Harbor: Cold Spring Harbor Laboratory, 1980), p. 167.

2. Ibid.

3. Chauncey Starr, "Social Benefit versus Technological Risk: What is our Society Reader to Pay for Safety?" *Science,* 165 (September 19, 1969), 1232-1238; Norman C. Rasmussen, *Reactor Safety Study: An Assessment of Accident Risks in U.S. Commercial Nuclear Power Plants* (Washington, D.C.: Nuclear Regulatory Commission, October 1975); William W. Lowrance, *Of Acceptable Risk: Science and the Determination of Safety* (Los Altos, Calif.: W. Kaufmann, 1976).

4. Daniel Kahneman and Amos Tversky, "Prospect Theory: An Analysis of Decision Under Risk," *Econometrica,* 47, 2 (March 1979), 263-291.

5. Simon Kuznets, assisted by Elisabeth Jenks, *Capital in the*

American Economy (Princeton, New Jersey: Princeton University Press, 1961), pp. 46-47.

6. Oscar Lewis, "The Culture of Poverty," *Scientific American* 215, 4 (October 1966), 19-25.

7. George Foster, "Peasant Society and the Image of the Limited Good," *American Anthropologist,* 55 (1965), 159-173.

8. Karl Mannheim, *Ideology and Utopia: An Introduction to the Sociology of Knowledge* (New York: Harcourt, Brace & Co., 1936; London: Routledge & Kegan Paul, 1960), pp. 106-107.

9. Louis Dumont, *Homo Hierarchicus,* English ed. (Weidenfeld & Nicolson, 1966), pp. xii, 105.

10. Mannheim, *Ideology and Utopia.* Mannheim makes a typology, describing organizations and their associated values and attitudes, but he does not explicitly take the next step of considering that the values might be the outcome of strategies for solving particular organizational problems.

11. Todd R. Laporte, *Organized Social Complexity: Challenge to Politics and Policy* (Princeton: Princeton University Press, 1975).

12. Mannheim, op. cit., p. 105.

13. Graham T. Allison, *The Essence of Decision: Explaining the Cuban Missile Crisis* (Boston: Little, Brown & Co., 1971).

14. See Aaron Wildavsky, "If Planning is Everything, Maybe It's Nothing," *Policy Sciences,* 4, 2 (June 1973), 127-153; and Naomi Caiden and Aaron Wildavsky, *Planning and Budgeting in Poor Countries* (New York: John Wiley & Sons, 1974; New Brunswick, New Jersey: Transaction, Inc., 1980).

15. Herbert Simon, *Models of Man* (New York: Wiley, 1957).

16. James Thompson and Arthur Tuden, "Strategies, Structures, and Processes of Organizational Decision," in *Comparative Studies in Administration* (Pittsburgh: University of Pittsburgh Press, 1959).

17. James March and Herbert Simon, *Organizations* (New York: Wiley, 1966).

18. Karl E. Weick, *The Social Psychology of Organizing,* 2d ed. (Reading, Mass.: Addison-Wesley Publishing Co., 1979).

19. Stafford Beer, *Designing Freedom* (London/New York/Sydney/Toronto: John Wiley & Sons, 1974).

20. For a public sector study, see Aaron Wildavsky, *The Politics of the Budgetary Process,* 3d ed. (Boston: Little, Brown & Co., 1979).

21. Allison, p. 88.

22. Bruce A. Ackerman, and William T. Hassler, "Beyond the

New Deal: Coal and the Clean Air Act," *The Yale Law Journal,* 89, 8 (July 1980), 1466-1571.

VI. The Border is Alarmed

1. E. Schweider, and D. Schweider, *A Peculiar People: Iowa's Old Order Amish* (Iowa State University Press, 1975), p. 51.
2. Frank H. Epp, *Mennonites in Canada 1786-1920: The History of a Separate People* (Macmillan of Canada, 1975), p. 115.
3. Schweider, *A Peculiar People,* p. 32.
4. Epp, *Mennonites,* pp. 260-261.
5. Ibid.
6. Schweider, *A Peculiar People,* p. 16.
7. Ibid., p. 51.
8. Joseph W. Eaton, and Albert J. Mayer, *Man's Capacity to Reproduce: The Demography of a Unique Population* (Glencoe, Ill.: Free Press, 1954).
9. David Flint, *The Hutterites: A Study in Prejudice* (Toronto: Oxford University Press, 1975), pp. 32, 95.
10. John Bennett, *Hutterian Brethren: The Agricultural Economy and Social Organization of a Communal People* (Stanford: Stanford University Press, 1967).
11. Flint, *The Hutterites,* p. 66.
12. Schweider, *A Peculiar People,* p. 72.
13. Ronald Knox, *Enthusiasm* (New York: Oxford University Press, 1950).
14. George Homans, *The Human Group* (New York: Harcourt Brace Jovanovich, 1950), p. 468.
15. Mark Holloway, *Heavens on Earth: Utopian Communities in America, 1680-1880* (New York: Dover Publications, 1951), p. 19; George Lockwood, *The New Harmony Movements* (New York: Dover Publications, 1905), p. 39.
16. Rosabeth Moss Kanter, *Commitment and Community: Communes and Utopias in Sociological Perspective* (Cambridge, Mass.: Harvard University Press, 1972).
17. Carol Weisbrod, *The Boundaries of Utopia* (New York: Pantheon, 1980), p. 223.
18. Ibid., chap. 14.

19. Richard H. Niebuhr, *The Social Sources of Denominationalism* (1st ed., 1929; New York, Meridian ed., World Publishing, 1957).

20. Bryan Wilson, ed., *Patterns of Sectarianism: organisation and ideology in social and religious movements* (London: Heineman, 1967).

21. Mancur Olson, *The Logic of Collective Action: Public Goods and the Theory of Groups,* Harvard Economic Studies (Cambridge, Mass.: Harvard University Press, 1965), refs. to 1971 paperback ed.

22. Ibid., p. 37, n. 56.

23. Veida Skultans, *Intimacy and Ritual: A Study of Spiritualism, Mediums and Groups* (London: Routledge & Kegan Paul, 1974), pp. 61-63.

24. Malcolm J. C. Calley, *God's People: West Indian Pentecostal Sects in England* (London, New York: Oxford University Press, 1965).

25. Ibid., pp. 46-47.

26. Ibid., p. 51.

27. Ibid., p. 57.

28. This is not to say that purity and impurity do not figure in nonsectarian types of church organization. The difference is in the expected source of impurity. In the case of New England Puritans who had early established a hierarchical form of society, the lower orders were impure. In the case of the true sectarian, wealth and power are the sources of impurity.

29. Ralph Waldo Emerson, "Nature," in *Emerson's Essays* (Dent: Everyman's Library, 1906).

VII. The Border Fears for Nature

(This chapter is based on research carried out by Andrée Breaux, Katherine Riggs, and Steve Rayner under the direction of Aaron Wildavsky and Mary Douglas.)

1. R. C. Mitchell, "National Environmental Lobbies and the Apparent Illogic of Collective Action," in *Collective Decision Making: Applications from Public Choice Theory,* ed. Clifford S. Russell (Baltimore and London: The Johns Hopkins University Press, 1979).

2. R. C. Mitchell, and J. Clarence Davies III, "The United States' Environmental Movement and Its Political Context: An Overview" (Discussion Paper 32 RFF Washington, D.C., 1978), p. 20.

3. William B. Devall, "The Governing of a Voluntary Organization: Oligarchy and Democracy in the Sierra Club" (Ph.D. diss., University of Oregon, 1970; Microfilm International, Ann Arbor, Michigan).

4. Paul Ehrlich, quoted in "Brower Power Awaits the Verdict," *Sports Illustrated,* 30 (April 14, 1969), 41.

5. Ibid., p. 38.

6. Robert A. Jones, "Fratricide in the Sierra Club," *The Nation,* 208, 18 (May 5, 1969), 569.

7. William B. Devall, "Brower Has an Active History," *Econews,* 10, 1 (January 1980), 11.

8. Hugh Nash, "Editorial," *Not Man Apart,* 2, 3 (March 1972), 3.

9. Ibid.

10. Tom Burke, "The Next Ten Years," *Not Man Apart,* 9, 10 (September 1979), p. 16.

11. Ann Roosevelt, "A Citizens' Appendix: How to Get Laws Introduced and Passed," in *Progress as if Survival Mattered* (San Francisco: Friends of the Earth, 1977), p. 306.

12. David Brower, "Muir and Friends," in *Not Man Apart,* 1, 1 (December 1970), 3-4.

13. "A Conversation with Gary Soucie," *Not Man Apart,* 1, 3 (February 1971), 10.

14. Alain Touraine, *La Prophetie Anti-Nucleaire* (Paris: Seuie, 1980).

15. Mary Douglas, "Cultural Bias" (Occasional Paper No. 35, Royal Anthropological Institute of Great Britain and Ireland, London, 1978).

16. Judith Johnsrud, "A Political Geography of the Nuclear Power Controversy: The Peaceful Atom in Pennsylvania" (Ph.D. diss., Pennsylvania State University, 1977).

17. Clamshell Alliance, "Declaration of Nuclear Resistance," in "How to Dig Clams," mimeographed, undated.

18. Ibid.

19. Alan Barry Sharaf, "Local Citizen Opposition to Nuclear Power Plants and Oil Refineries" (Ph.D. diss., Clark University, Worcester, Massachusetts, 1978).

20. *It's About Times* (August 1979), p. 5.

21. Stephen Zunes, "Seabrook: A Turning Point," *Progressive,* 42, 9 (September 1978), 30.

22. *It's About Times* (June-July 1979), p. 3.

23. *It's About Times* (February 1980), p. 2.

24. Quoted in Joan Sweeney, "A-Protesters: Single Issue Many Groups," *Los Angeles Times* (November 18, 1979).

25. Tracy Kidder, "The Nonviolent War Against Nuclear Power," *Atlantic* (September 1978), p. 75.

26. *It's About Times* (September 1979), p. 5.

27. *It's About Times* (December-January 1979), p. 2.

28. Harvey Wasserman, "The Clamshell Alliance: Getting it Together," *Progressive,* 41, 9 (September 1977), 18.

29. For a detailed account of how this kind of fieldwork could be conducted, see Steve Rayner and Jonathan Gross, *A Handbook for Grid/Group Analysis,* forthcoming.

VIII. America is a Border Country

1. David Vogel, "The Public-Interest Movement and the American Reform Tradition," *The Political Science Quarterly,* 95, 4 (Winter 1980-1981), 607-627. Vogel cites *The Federalist Papers,* ed. Roy P. Fairfield (Garden City, N.Y.: Doubleday and Co., 1961); Robert Dahl, *Who Governs?* (New Haven, Conn.: Yale University Press, 1961); Daniel Boorstin, *The Genius of American Politics* (Chicago: University of Chicago Press, 1953), p. 616.

2. Austin Ranney, *Curing the Mischiefs of Faction* (Berkeley, Los Angeles, London: University of California Press, 1975).

3. Alexis de Tocqueville, *Democracy in America* (New York: Alfred A. Knopf, Vintage Books, 1945).

4. Vogel, "The Public-Interest Movement," p. 608.

5. Daniel Mazmanian and Paul Sabatier, "The Attitudes of an Administrative Elite: The Commissioners and Staffs of the California Coastal Commissions" (Paper presented at the Western Political Science Association, San Francisco, April 1976).

6. James Q. Wilson, *The Amateur Democrat* (Chicago: University of Chicago Press, 1966).

7. Aaron Wildavsky, "The Goldwater Phenomenon: Purists, Politicians, and the Two-Party System," *Review of Politics,* 27 (July 1965), 386-413.

8. Aaron Wildavsky, "The Meaning of 'Youth' in the Struggle for Control of the Democratic Party," in *The Revolt Against the Masses* (New York: Basic Books, 1971), pp. 270-287.

9. These changes are discussed in the various editions of Nelson Polsby and Aaron Wildavsky, *Presidential Elections*, 5th ed. (New York: Scribner's, 1979).

10. Andrew McFarland, "Recent Social Movements and Theories of Power in America" (Paper prepared for Annual Meeting of The American Political Science Association, August 31, 1979, Washington, D.C.).

11. Joseph A. Schumpeter, *Capitalism, Socialism and Democracy* (New York: Harper & Row, 1942), pp. 144, 145.

12. See Victor Fuchs (assisted by Irving Leurson), *The Service Economy* (New York: National Bureau of Economic Research, 1968); "Economic Growth and the Rise of Service Employment," National Bureau of Economic Research, Working Paper, No. 486, June 1980.

13. Isaiah Berlin claims the Russians "invented social criticism" of the kind that merges life and art, making one into a perpetual criticism of the other. "The phenomenon itself," Berlin concludes ([the intelligentsia] "conceived themselves as being a dedicated order, almost a secular priesthood, devoted to the spreading of a specific attitude to life, something like a gospel."), "with its . . . revolutionary consequences is, I suppose, the largest single Russian contribution to social change in the world." Isaiah Berlin, *Russian Thinkers* (New York: Penguin Books, 1979), pp. 116-117.

14. Denton E. Morrison, "The Environmental Movement: Conflict Dynamics," *Journal of Voluntary Action Research*, 2 (April 1973), 74-85. A more direct theory of interest in the environment has been proposed by Morrison: "Whatever relationships of antagonism and exploitation exist between the various strata of ownership, control, and wealth in modern industrial capitalism, *all* who are tied to this system share, to the extent that their ties are direct and to those segments of the economy most visibly involved in environmental exploitation, a common fate and a common interest in continued environmental exploitation. This suggests, in contrast with Marxist and other more general notions of class antagonism, that many of the important industrial conflicts emerging in this country around environmental issues . . . [are] between *all* those associated directly with industries threatened by the costs of environmental reform and those

who push those reforms, the environmentalists." His hypothesis is that it is not class conflict, but conflict between those in and out of industry that matters.

15. *New Society* (March 22, 1979), p. 683.

16. Robert Nathan Mayer, "The Social Bases of Environmental Opinion" (Ph.D. diss., University of California at Berkeley, 1978), p. 269.

17. Allan Malkis and Harold G. Malkis, "Support for the Ideology of the Environmental Movement: Tests of Alternative Hypotheses," *Western Sociological Review*, 8 (1977), 25-47.

18. Gunnar Myrdal, *An American Dilemma* (New York/London: Harper & Bros., 1944).

19. Gary Orfield, *Congressional Power: Congress and Social Change* (New York: Harcourt Brace Jovanovich, 1975).

20. Andrew S. McFarland, "Recent Social Movements and Theories of Power in America" (Paper prepared for the 1979 Annual Meeting of the American Political Science Association, Washington, D.C., August 31, 1979).

21. Emily Stoper, "The Student Non-Violent Coordinating Committee: Rise and Fall of a Redemptive Organization," *Journal of Black Studies*, 3, 1 (September 1977), 13-33.

22. See Aaron Wildavsky, "The Empty-head Blues: Black Rebellion and White Reaction," *The Public Interest*, 11 (Spring 1968), pp. 3-16; and "The Search for the Oppressed," *Freedom at Issue*, no. 16 (November/December 1972), pp. 5-16.

23. Jeffrey N. Berry, *Lobbying for the People: The Political Behavior of Public Interest Groups* (Princeton: Princeton University Press, 1977), p. 7.

24. Vogel, *The Public-Interest Movement*, p. 621.

25. The Center for Responsive Governance and The Interagency Council on Citizen Participation, "Financing Public Interest Advocacy," MSS-80-10 (October 1980), pp. 8-10.

26. Council on Environmental Quality, *Environmental Quality-1975* (Washington, D.C.: U.S. Government Printing Office, 1975).

27. Berry, *Lobbying for the People*, p. 109.

28. Ibid., pp. 209-210.

29. Ibid.

30. Mitchell, "National Environmental Lobbies," p. 100.

31. Ibid., pp. 113-114.

212   *Notes to Pages 171-182*

32. Karl R. Popper and John C. Eccles, *The Self and Its Brain* (Berlin/New York/London: Springer International, 1977), p. 8.

33. See Jo Freeman's outstanding *The Politics of Women's Liberation* (New York: Longman, 1975).

IX. The Dialogue is Political

1. See Michael Thompson, chapters in *Essays in the Sociology of Perception* (forthcoming in 1982, London, Routledge & Kegan Paul). To complete the view of the cultural horizon, two more possibilities should be mentioned, both ways of not choosing either center or border and therefore not pertinent to political questions: one is a negative position, unaligned by default, and the other a positive position, unaligned by commitment. No one can try to follow the former because trying is ruled out by definition. Taking a negative or uncommitted attitude toward society's options, such a person will become subject to rules made by others determined to put some rational coherence into their lives. Though he is sure to be manipulated and constrained, he can still go on treating all information as equally important and unimportant, never imposing a principle of selection or developing a consistent set of goals. This absence of focus contrasts with the other kind of nonalignment that is a systematic commitment to noncommitment. The latter requires a sustained effort to create a kind of society in which no options are finally closed and no individuals are allowed to exert power over others.

2. See Peter Berger, *The Social Reality of Religion* (London: Faber and Faber, 1969. [U.S. title, *The Sacred Canopy*]), on "theodicy.

3. Douglas L. Oliver, *A Solomon Island Society: Kinship and Leadership Among the Sinai of Bougainville* (London: Oxford University Press, 1957).

4. There is no difficulty in dealing with the failures of various kinds if the philosophy allows slavery or the killing of captives.

5. See Stanley Lebergott, *The American Economy: Income, Wealth, and Want* (Princeton: Princeton University Press, 1976), p. 57.

6. Andrew S. McFarland, *Public Interest Lobbies: Decision Making on Energy* (Washington, D.C.: American Enterprise Institute, 1976), pp. 6-12; and *Common Cause* (unpublished manuscript).

Conclusion: Risk is a Collective Construct

1. Mary Douglas, "Cultural Bias."

2. Steve Rayner and Jonathan Gross, *Handbook for Grid-Group Analysis* (forthcoming).

3. William C. Clark, "Witches, Floods, and Wonder Drugs: Historical Perspectives on Risk Management," Paper for Symposium on Societal Risk Assessment: How Safe Is Safe Enough?, sponsored by General Motors Corporation, October 1979.

4. C. S. Holling, "Resilience and Stability of Ecological Systems," *Annual Review of Ecology and Systematics,* 4 (1973), 1-23.

Index

Abalone Alliance, 142, 144, 146. *See also* Antinuclear movement

Acceptable risk. *See* Risk, acceptability of

Accountability, 7, 20-21, 29-31, 33-35, 38-39, 40, 75, 100, 190

Affinity groups, 145, 148. *See also* Antinuclear movement; Sectarianism

Amish, 14, 124; as border, 104-106, 110, 111; egalitarianism of, 105, 107; reject technology, 105, 107; risk perception of, 105-106, 107-108

Amman, Jacob, 105

Anabaptists, 104-111. *See also* Amish; Hutterites

Antinuclear movement, 61, 124, 137-138, 139-151; Abalone Alliance as, 142, 144, 146; Clamshell Alliance as, 142-143, 145, 147-149, 150; ECNP as, 140-141, 147-149; direct-action groups of, 142-143, 144, 145; grid/group analysis of, 139-140, 148-149, 150; history of, 139-140; leaders of, 148; local intervener groups in, 140-142, 143, 144, 147, 148, 149; membership of, 140, 141, 142-143; in Pennsylvania, 140; and politics, 144; as sectarian, 137-138, 139, 143. *See also* Nuclear power

Articles of Confederation, 153

Atomic Energy Commission, 61, 140

Bias, cultural, and risk, 8-9, 14-15, 29-31, 61, 88-89, 149, 150-151, 175-185, 191-193, 195

Blame. *See* Accountability

Border, 101, 177; alarm of, 102-125; Amish as, 104-106, 110, 111; Anabaptists as, 104-111; bureaucracy in, 103; and center, 81, 103, 121-122, 167, 173, 174-185; claims of, 189; concept of, 103; dilemma of, 138; direct-action groups in, 142-143, 144, 145-147, 149; egalitarianism of, 145, 146, 147, 150, 177; in environmental movement, 126-151; Friends of the Earth as, 137; growth of, 172-173; hierarchy in, 103; Hutterites as, 104, 105; intelligentsia as, 160-161; local

intervener groups as, 140-142,
143, 144, 147-148, 149; pessimism of, 190-191; politics of,
137, 169; public interest groups
as, 164-173; and risk, 81, 102,
122, 174-175, 188-189, 191; as
sectarian, 174; and service industries, 159-160; strategy, 137;
United States as, 152-173; views
of, 122-123, 126, 150-151, 182;
voice of, 81, 103-104, 126, 130,
181; voluntariness of, 103-104,
120, 189. *See also* Amish; Antinuclear movement; Friends of
the Earth; Sectarianism; Voluntariness
Brower, David: and Friends of the
Earth, 132-134; and Sierra Club,
130-132, 134
Brown, Edmund G., Jr., 144
Bureaucracy. *See* Hierarchy

Cancer: concern about, 54-55; and
diet, 57; and drinking water, 50,
51-52; environmentally caused,
55, 56-58; risk of, 7, 54; and
smoking, 55. *See also* Carcinogens
Capitalism, 158
Carcinogens, 17, 55-56; studies of,
58-59; tests for, 54; in water, 50-
53. *See also* Cancer
Carson, Rachel, 128
Censorship, 180, 182
Center, 47, 83-101, 102, 120, 123,
172, 177, 183; attacked, 121,
125, 182; and border, 81, 103,
121-122, 167, 173, 174-185;
claims of, 189; factionalism in,
154; hierarchy as, 174, 175; market as, 174, 175; need for, 182; as
optimistic, 122, 191; production
industry as, 160; and risk, 101,
122, 174-175, 188-189; and sectarianism, 165, 166, 173, 182,
183; strategy, 137; in United
States, 153-154, 162, 183. *See*

also Hierarchy; Market individualism
Center for Disease Control, 60
Chemicals, 1, 2, 3; as carcinogens,
53; synthetic, 53; in water, 51-52
Choice, rational, 72-73, 81, 82,
101; constraints on, 77, 78; fac-
tors in, 77-78, 83-85; morality in,
83-84; probability in, 78-79, 80;
and risk, 74-75, 76-77. *See also*
Decision-making
Civil rights movement, 162, 163-
164, 173
Clamshell Alliance, 142-143, 145,
150; and ECNP, 147-149. *See*
also Antinuclear movement
Coal, as pollutant, 71, 97-98
Collectivism. *See* Hierarchy; Hut-
terites
Common Cause, 172, 182
Computers, 83
Consent: informed, 34; in risk, 5-6
Conservation. *See* Environment;
Environmental movement
Construct, collective, risk as, 186-
198
Cost-benefit analysis, 88; of risk
assessment, 68, 69-70, 71
Costle, Douglas M., 51, 53
Crime, risk of, 2, 3, 44
Critical Mass, 141

Danger. *See* Risk
Death: infant, 2, 35, 39, 59-60;
natural, 31, 32, 33
Decision-making, 77-79, 109-110,
113; by consensus, 145-146, 147;
in hierarchy, 91-94; role of institutions in, 80, 81, 85, 88-89, 90-
91, 100; and risk, 83, 93-94. *See*
also Choice, rational
Disfellowship, 119. *See also* Factionalism; Sectarianism, schism in
Disobedience, civil, 142

Earth Day (1970), 128
Ecology movement, 58, 138, 151.

See also Environment; Environmental movement

Economy: as frontier, 183, 184; and growth of environmental concern, 159-160, 161; sectarianism on, 183, 184

Education, 6, 12, 13, 159-160

Egalitarianism, 154; of Amish, 105, 107; in border groups, 145, 146, 147, 150, 177; and hierarchy, 91, 179-180; and institutions, 176-180; and market, 178-179, 180; in sectarianism, 10, 117, 118, 119, 126, 133, 139, 144-145, 146, 147, 149-150, 156, 163-164, 177, 178, 180, 191

Energy, 2

Environment, 54, 77; and cancer, 55-58; concern for, 12, 14, 16, 17, 24, 44, 47, 62-63, 125, 128-151, 155, 161, 162-163, 194; hazards of, 55-58, 65; Higginson on, 56-58; and politics, 98, 155, 163. *See also* Antinuclear movement; Environmental movement

Environmental Coalition on Nuclear Power (ECNP), 140-141, 147-149

Environmental Defense Fund, 129

Environmental movement, 124, 186, 188, 196; as border, 126-151; as hierarchy, 130; leadership of, 131-133, 145, 146, 147, 148-149, 164; lobbying by, 129, 130, 171; membership of, 129-130, 170-171; multiplicity of, 134-135. *See also* Antinuclear movement; Friends of the Earth; National Audubon Society; Sierra Club

Environmental Protection Agency, 97, 98; and drinking water, 50-53

Envy, 176; in market, 178-179; in sectarianism, 177

Factionalism: in center, 154; in politics, 154-157. *See also* Sectarianism, schism in

Fear, 8, 10; in market, 96; and risk, 2, 6, 7

Federalist Papers, The, 154

Friends of the Earth, 132-137, 161; aims of, 135, 136, 137; as border, 137; as sectarian, 132-137; and Sierra Club, 137, 139; support for, 135-136; as voluntary group, 132-134

Frontier, 155; as safety valve, 183

Future: as border/center issue, 122; concern for, 23, 97; hierarchy on, 99-100; market individualism on, 99-100; and risk perception, 85-87; sectarianism on, 127

Goldwater, Barry, 156

Grid/group analysis, 138-139; of antinuclear movement, 139-140, 148-149, 150

Handler, Philip: on carcinogens, 55-56; on estimation of risk, 65-66

Harris polls, 2, 44

Hierarchy, 102, 114, 121, 122, 124, 138, 139, 171, 172, 173; accountability in, 100; in border, 103; bureaucracy in, 183, 184, 185; censorship in, 180; as center, 174, 175; collectivism in, 115-117, 120; compromise in, 91; and decision-making, 91-94; defects of, 190; egalitarianism of, 91, 179-180; environmental groups as, 130; fears of, 187; on future, 99-100; Hutterites as, 108-111; maintenance of, 126-127; vs. market, 90, 98-99, 100, 181; as optimistic, 191; and politics, 98, 156-157, 181; in production process, 161; risk perception of, 90-94, 95, 96, 97, 100, 101, 188; and safety, 161; and sectarianism, 124, 181; and service industries, 160; Shakers as, 113; Sierra Club as, 129, 130, 131; in United

States, 156-157, 183. *See also* Center

Higginson, John, 56-58

Hima, of Uganda, 40-48, 107

Hutter, Jacob, 104

Hutterites, 14, 124; as border, 104, 105; as hierarchy, 108-111. *See also* Amish

Individualism. *See* Market individualism

Industry, 160, 161

Inequality, social, 176-180

Institutions: decision-making role of, 80, 81, 85, 88-89, 90-91, 100; and risk, 80, 81, 88-89; and social inequality, 176-180

Insurance, and risk assessment, 74-75, 76

Iru, of Uganda, 42, 43, 46-47

It's About Times, 146

Knowledge: imperfect, 74, 75-76, 193; and risk, 1-6, 18, 74, 75-76, 80-81, 192-193

Lévy-Bruhl, Lucien, 31-32, 39

Liability. *See* Accountability

Life expectancy, 2, 32, 45, 184-185

Lobbying, 117, 165; environmental, 129, 130, 171; federal support of, 167

McCarthy, Eugene, 156

Madison, James, 154

Malpractice, 33-35

Market individualism, 95-101, 102, 117, 121, 138-139, 158, 163, 184, 185, 189, 190; as center, 174, 175; and cost-benefit analysis, 68, 71; in danger, 181; defects of, 190; egalitarianism of, 178-179, 180; fears of, 96; on future, 99-100; goals of, 95-96; vs. hierarchy, 90, 98-99, 100, 181; as optimistic, 191; Populists on, 157; risk perception of, 28, 90, 94, 95-96, 97-99, 100, 101, 188;

success in, 179; and time, 96; views of, 101, 178-179

Maslow theory of wants, 12, 13

Mead, Margaret, 61-62

Membership, mail-order, 165, 167, 168, 169-170, 173

Morality: in choice, 83-84; and risk, 7, 8, 29-31, 33

Nader, Ralph, 141

National Audubon Society, 129, 130, 142

National Wildlife Federation, 129

Natural standards, 47-48, 69, 71

Nature. *See* Environment

Normality. *See* Statistical normality

Nuclear power, 33, 140-141, 147-149; risks of, 1, 59-61, 65. *See also* Antinuclear movement

Nuclear Regulatory Commission, 140

Occupational Safety and Health Administration, 53

Perception. *See* Risk perception

Politics: and antinuclear movement, 144; of border, 137, 169; and environment, 98, 155, 163; factionalism in, 154-157; in hierarchy, 98, 156-157, 181; participation in, 154-155; risk and, 4, 7-8, 17, 19, 64, 65-66, 73-74, 90-92, 184-185; and sectarianism, 154-156, 181-185

Pollution, 3, 128; air, 44-45, 63, 97-99; beliefs, 35-40, 45, 46, 47; concern for, 10, 124, 125, 161; environmental, 97, 98; man-made, 58; movement against, 98-99, 163; nontechnical, 36-40; and purity, 36-37; risks of, 1, 2, 7, 8; sexual, 37-38, 39-40; technical, 36; water, 50, 51-52, 129. *See also* Environmental movement

Populists, 157

Poverty, 122, 124

Preference: expressed, 69, 70, 71, 76; revealed, 68-69, 70, 71, 76
Probability, 71, 75, 76, 83, 84, 85, 87, 89, 195; in rational choice, 78-79, 80; and risk, 21-22, 100, 187
Progressive Era, 155, 157
Public goods, 115-118, 170
Public interest groups, 12, 13, 182; as border, 164-173; leaders of, 168; membership of, 170-171; problems of, 172; as sectarian, 164-173; support for, 166-167; lack of structure of, 171-172
Public interest law, 166
Purity, 47, 156; and pollution, 36-37; and sectarianism, 10, 122, 124, 127, 139, 156, 168

Radiation, 65
Rationality: bounded, 77; sectarian, 104
Reflection effect, 78, 79
Regulation: of carcinogens, 55; cost of, 50-51; government, 21; need for, 23; of risk, 19, 20, 24-26, 53-54, 58, 74-75, 183-184
Relativism, 186-187, 188, 191-192, 195
Risk: acceptability of, 4, 6, 9-10, 64, 65-66, 188, 194; accountability for, 7, 20-21, 29-31, 33-35, 38-39, 40, 75, 100, 190; American focus on, 10-11, 152-173; attitudes toward, 2, 29-32, 87-101, 193, 194; aversion, 8, 9, 11, 16, 18, 21-22, 27-28, 67, 79, 81, 100, 194, 195; and border, 81, 102, 122, 174-175, 188-189, 191; of cancer, 7, 54; and center, 101, 122, 174-175, 188-189; and choice, 74-75, 76-77; as collective construct, 186-198; consent in, 5-6, 34; cultural biases and, 8-9, 14-15, 29-31, 61, 88-89, 149, 150-151, 175-185, 191-193, 195; and decision-making, 83, 93-94; disagreement on, 49-66, 193; and

education, 12, 13; external, 180, 181; fear of, 2, 6, 7, 8, 10, hidden, 16-29; and institutions, 80, 81, 88-89; involuntary, 16-21, 26, 190; irreversible, 16, 21-28; knowledge of, 1-6, 18, 74, 75-76, 80-81, 192-193; management, 195-198; medical, 33-35; and moral responsibility, 7, 8, 29-31, 33; and politics, 4, 7-8, 17, 19, 64, 65-66, 73-74, 90-92, 184-185; of pollution, 1, 2, 7, 8; prevention, 183; and probability, 21-22, 100, 187; problems of, 5-6; reduction of, 1, 4; regulation of, 19, 20, 24-26, 53-54, 58, 74-75, 183-184; schism as, 111, 112; selection, 7, 8, 9, 14, 15, 19, 29-48, 72-73, 84-85, 87, 93-94, 126, 176, 187, 197-198; societal factors of, 8, 89-90; taking, 8, 9, 21-22, 28, 67, 99, 100, 190, 194; and technology, 1-2, 9-10, 13, 14, 16, 17, 32-35, 74, 124, 139, 151; temporal aspects of, 85, 86-87, 89, 99-100; and trust, 34, 89; types of, 1, 2, 3, 187; and uncertainty, 4-5, 21-22, 78, 79, 86; voluntary, 17, 18-20, 75. *See also* Risk assessment; Risk perception
Risk assessment, 3-5, 14, 28, 65-66, 67-82, 89, 194-195; by business, 92-93; cost-benefit analysis and, 68, 69-70, 71, 88; data, too much in, 71-72; education and, 6; expressed preference method of, 69, 70, 71, 76; and imperfect knowledge, 80-81; natural standards method of, 69, 71; objectivity in, 68-73; revealed preference method of, 68-69, 70, 71, 76; subjectivity in, 68-73; techniques, 67-68
Risk-benefit analysis, 17-19, 51, 52, 65-66
Risk perception, 6, 7-15, 43-44, 61, 79-80, 126, 180, 181, 185, 188-189, 193-194; of Amish, 105-106,

107-108; future considered in, 85-87; hierarchy and, 90-94, 95, 96, 97-99, 100, 101, 188; of market individualism, 28, 90, 94, 95-96, 97-99, 100, 101, 188; modern vs. premodern, 29-32; and moral judgment, 30-31; of sectarianism, 188; social influences on, 9, 61, 83-85; and technology, 9-10
Risk-utility analysis. *See* Cost-benefit analysis
Roosevelt, Theodore, 128
Russia, intelligentsia of, 160-161

Safety, concern for, 11-12, 18-19, 27-28, 53, 149, 161, 195, 196
Seabrook, New Hampshire, 142-143
Science: disagrees on risk, 49-66; politicized, 64-66
Sectarianism, 114-115, 116-125, 130; antinuclear movement as, 137-138, 139, 143; border as, 174; and center, 165, 166, 173, 182, 183; contradictions in, 177-178; cosmology of, 127, 137; described, 139, 146; dilemma of, 124, 183; on economy, 183, 184; egalitarianism of, 10, 117, 118, 119, 126, 133, 139, 144-145, 146, 147, 149-150, 156, 163-164, 177, 178, 180, 191; and environmental concern, 163; failings of, 190; fear of infiltration of, 121, 123-124, 133, 135, 139, 153; in Friends of the Earth, 132-137; future and, 127; and government, 165, 183, 184; group size in, 110, 112, 116, 120, 123, 129, 136, 139, 141, 146; growth of, 14, 152, 157, 158; and hierarchy, 124, 181; and human goodness, 10, 122-123, 124, 127, 169, 177, 178, 180; ideal, 10-11; invokes danger, 127; lack of structure in, 171-172; lack of trust in, 162; leadership of, 120, 167, 168, 172;

participation in, 117-119, 120; pessimism of, 122, 190-191; and politics, 154-156, 181-185; poverty in, 121, 124; public interest groups as, 164-173; and purity, 10, 122, 124, 127, 139, 156, 168; restraints on, 167; risk perception of, 188; and risk selection, 14; schism in, 111, 112, 118-120, 123, 146-147, 182-183; in United States, 152-173; views of, 177-178, 187; wealth rejected by, 11; worldliness rejected by, 121, 123, 127. *See also* Border
Service industries, 159-160
Shakers, 113
Sierra Club, 128, 133, 172; and Friends of the Earth, 137, 139; as hierarchy, 129, 130, 131; lobbying by, 130; split in, 130-132, 134; as voluntary group, 132
Social organization. *See* Border; Center; Hierarchy; Market individualism; Sectarianism
Spiritualism, 118
Starr, Chauncey, 17-19
Statistical normality, 59-60
Superstition, 29, 31

Technology, 16-29, 35, 194; assessment, 81-82; benefits of, 45-46; disputes over, 49-50, 67; Hutterites accept, 111; misuse of, 24-25; rejection of, 105, 107, 149, 182; and risk, 1-2, 9-10, 13, 14, 16, 17, 32-35, 74, 124, 139, 151; risk-benefit analysis of, 17, 51, 52; and wealth, 124; and what is normal, 32-35, 36
Three Mile Island, 59, 60
Time: market attitude toward, 96; as factor of risk, 85, 86-87, 89, 99-100
Tocqueville, Alexis de, 154
Trust, 34, 89, 162

Uncertainty: as opportunity, 96; and risk, 4-5, 21-22, 78, 79, 86

United States: as border, 152-173; center in, 153-154, 162, 183; concern for nature, 126-151; Constitution, 153, 157; and democracies, 158-159; hierarchy in, 156-157, 183; higher education in, 159-160; risk concerns of, 8, 10-11, 15, 16, 151, 152-173; sectarianism in, 152-173
Utopian communities, 112-113

Vietnam War, 162, 173
Violence, 178
Voluntariness, 114, 116-125, 126, 153, 164-165; and border, 103-104, 120, 189; dilemmas of, 115-121, 127; in environmental movement, 128-129, 132-134; and public goods, 116-117

War, risk of, 2, 3
Water: movement for clean, 50-53; pollution, 129
Watergate, 162
Wealth: and envy, 179, 180; rejected, 11; and technology, 124
Witchcraft, 38-42 passim
Worldliness, 106-107; as dangerous, 10-11; rejected by sectarians, 121, 123, 127

Designer:	UC Press Staff
Compositor:	Janet Sheila Brown
Printer:	Vail-Ballou Press
Binder:	Vail-Ballou Press
Text:	Baskerville 11/13
Display:	Baskerville 18 pt
	Baskerville Chapter titles 22 pt.